Contents

Preface

This book is aimed primarily at undergraduate students on fashion and textiles-related courses, lecturers and careers advisers, as well as those already working within fashion and textiles who are considering their next career move. It is intended to represent as wide a range of relevant jobs as is reasonably possible with case studies of people at different levels across the UK, within the given time constraints and scope of the book. The aim is to widen readers' knowledge of career options from the partial and limited perception of the fashion industry often portrayed in the media. The emphasis on companies in London within the book is intentional as London remains the creative and organisational hub of fashion and textiles. However, jobs in every field in this book are available in various parts of the country. By looking at the details of these key roles it is possible to build up a picture of how the fashion and textiles industry currently operates in the UK and the integration between the different jobs, companies and industry sectors. All interviews for the case studies were carried out during 2005.

The book gives a comprehensive view of fashion and textiles roles, but is not completely exhaustive as the aim is to strike a balance between the careers which fashion and textiles graduates realistically pursue and the employment demands of the industry in which they aim to work. Accordingly, references to textiles within this book are restricted to fashion-orientated end uses, although there are various other significant markets for textiles, including interiors and the automotive industry. The fields of fashion photography and modelling have not been covered as they are well documented elsewhere and are not typical careers for fashion and textiles graduates.

Acknowledgements

Thanks to all of the people who were interviewed or contributed quotes for this book. I am amazed that so many people were willing to give their valuable time. Particular thanks go to Helen Kenny who contributed three chapters: Fashion PR, Fashion Journalism and Fashion Styling, giving an additional perspective through her own experience of how the world of fashion operates and influencing the overall style and structure of the book. I would like to thank Dr Amanda Briggs-Goode who has been involved throughout the progress of the book, providing advice regarding textile design.

A variety of people supplied me with images featured in the book or relevant contacts, and without their help the content would not have been so diverse: Winifred Aldrich; Esme Baker; Janet Biggs; Cecilia Black; Hilary Carlisle; Sue Cassie; Sally Denton; Becky Ferrier; Ben Fleming; Jess Fountain; Andrew Grimes; Cécile Harari-Alle; Yvonne Heinen; Stephen Higginson; Lisa Hilliard; Louise Housley; Tracey Jacob; Hasmita Jesani; Robin Lewis; Sue Lloyd; Wendy Malem; Eric Musgrave; Carrie Neale; Kelly Owens; Donna Paterson; Emma Price; Sean Price; Julia Richards; Alannah Weston and Kerry Wilson. The following colleagues at NTU supported me in various ways, by reading drafts of my text or supplying images, contacts or information: Jane Bartholomew; Sue Beckett; Linda Brown; Maggie Bushby; Carol Cloughton; Rosemarie Goulding; Fiona Hamblin; Karen Harrigan; Katie Holbrook; Alistair Knox; Sandra McNabb; Jo O'Rourke; Gillian Proctor and Angela Vesey. NTU students Martha Ferguson; Anna Frendo; Tamsin Lever; Rebecca Plummer and Abigail Jordan read drafts to check that the style was student-friendly. Finally, thanks to Dave and my Mum for enabling me to find time for research and writing.

Helen Goworek

Introduction

Fashion design is the most well-known and coveted career in the fashion and textiles business. Fashion designers are often perceived as being rich, famous and constantly rubbing shoulders with celebrities. Whilst this is true of some of the big catwalk names, there are many thousands of employees in this massive business who work behind the scenes and do not receive the acclaim and wealth of Donna Karan or Alexander McQueen. Without these crucial supporting roles the fashion and textiles industry would not exist. Working in the fashion industry is unlikely to make you rich or famous but there is a realistic chance of gaining a reasonably paid, interesting career, if you are sufficiently hard-working, creative and self-motivated. The aim of this book is to create an awareness of the extensive range of jobs that are available within fashion and textiles, and to outline the responsibilities involved in many of these roles.

The retail clothing market is a significant sector of the UK economy, estimated by Mintel to have been worth £37 billion in 2004, with womenswear unsurprisingly selling higher volumes than menswear and childrenswear combined. Many clothing stores have expanded the number of their outlets in this country since 2000. Consequently fashion retailers, the fabric and garment suppliers who produce their merchandise and the publications in which it is promoted are major sources of employment.

How does the concept in a designer's sketchbook turn into the reality of the product which is sold by a fashion retailer? Many people in various roles, often from several different countries, are responsible for taking care of the product during the numerous stages through which it must travel in order for it to eventually arrive in store. Figure 1.1 shows a simplistic version of the supply chain for fashion products, each sector providing a variety of design, technical and sales positions which are explained further within the book.

Whilst designers can be credited with supplying the creative inspiration behind fashion and textiles products, other people also use creative and technical skills to turn these original ideas into tangible products to be purchased by the customer.

1

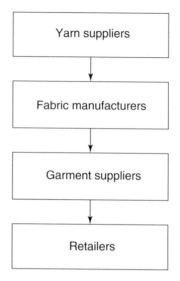

Fig. 1.1 The fashion and textiles supply chain

Fashion and textile designers are undoubtedly essential participants in the early stages of the chain of events which leads to products being manufactured and sold. Have you ever considered the journey that a garment takes before it arrives in a store? Who decides how many of this style will be made, in which colours? Who decides what date it will be delivered and exactly where it will be located on the shop floor? Who specifies the washing instructions and how much it will sell for? For every garment in a store, decisions need to be made on which trimmings to use and which supplier will manufacture it in which country. These vital decisions are made by teams of people in retailers and manufacturers working together including buyers, fabric technologists and visual merchandisers.

The fashion and textiles industry operates on a global scale. Many UK store groups have rising numbers of branches abroad and equally, retailers from other countries have made inroads into the UK fashion market including Spanish retailers Zara and Mango, Swedish chain H&M and American retail giant Gap. In contrast to other European countries, the UK fashion market is dominated by specialist clothing chains, notably the three major store groups: Marks & Spencer, Next and the Arcadia Group.

The vast majority of fashion and textiles products sold in the UK are manufactured overseas. The main sources of clothing imports are the Far East, India, Bangladesh, Turkey and Eastern Europe (Mintel, 2005). This is one of the factors that has led to diminishing quantities of textiles and clothing being produced in the UK and a sharp reduction in the numbers employed in fabric and garment manufacture. However, the design, development and sales of fashion products remain largely in this country, separate from the manufacturing base. According to the academic careers website prospects.ac.uk:

Given the move of the (fashion and textiles) industry away from a mainly manufac-turing focus, there is probably wider scope for graduate careers than ever before, despite the contraction in overall employment.

A major British export is the constant flow of fashion and textile design graduates who are employed by companies abroad. Alice Smith, director of fashion recruit-ment agency Smith and Pye stated in an interview with *Drapers* in 2005:

It is a little known fact outside of the industry that all the big name designers in the Europe and US have creative teams made up of designers from all levels of experience who are from UK universities and colleges. (p.24)

Boundaries are blurring between different jobs and even industries and it is pos-sible to swap fashion and textiles careers. Fashion journalist Luella Bartley and illustrator Julie Verhoeven have designed catwalk collections and innumerable pop stars have launched eponymous designer labels. Case studies have been included in each job-related chapter to offer valuable examples of current practice and possible career paths. It was difficult to categorise the job roles of some of the interviewees featured because they had transferred from one career to another, which is indicative of the industry as a whole. If you decide to pursue a career in fashion and textiles it is helpful to have an appreciation of the other roles with whom you will liaise. Chapters run in a consecutive order based broadly on the handover of products from one role to another. Salary ranges have not been specif-ically mentioned because they vary between companies and change from one year to the next, but there are some guidelines about how salaries compare in differ-ent jobs. A general rule is that for a similar type of job title you are likely to be paid more by a high street retailer or manufacturer than a designer-level company. This may be the reverse of general expectations but the size of the company is more of an indication of the salary level than the selling price of their products.

Jobs in fashion retailing include:

- retail managers;
- sales advisers;
- personal shoppers;
- buyers;
- merchandisers;
- fashion designers;
- fabric technologists;
- garment technologists;
- visual merchandisers.

Fabric and garment suppliers employ:

- textile designers;
- fashion designers;
- pattern cutters;

- sales representatives;
- fabric technologists;
- garment technologists.

The main roles in fashion media are:

- fashion journalists;
- fashion PRs;
- fashion stylists;
- fashion forecasters;
- fashion illustrators.

Realistically, many entry level jobs such as trainee or assistant can be administrative and repetitive but it is worth sticking with them as, once promoted, more responsibility and diversity will be available in a more senior role. Wages increase with promotion and company cars are offered with many of the jobs detailed here, after progressing above trainee or assistant level, as most involve travelling regularly in the UK. Many jobs for suppliers and retailers include overseas travel to source products and inspiration. There are many different routes into careers in fashion and textiles, demonstrated by the case studies within the chapters.

FURTHER READING

Mintel (2005) Men's Outerwear – UK. Mintel, London
Retail Intelligence (2005) Clothing Retailing. Mintel, London.
Smith, A. (2005) in Anderson, A. Designing your career. *Drapers*, 28 May 2005, p. 24.
www.prospects.ac.uk

Textile design

2

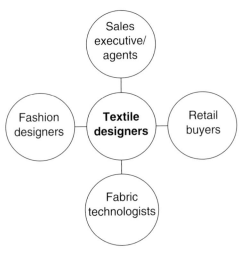

Fig. 2.1 Liaison between textile designers and other roles

Textile design is a large sphere of employment, incorporating the design of printed, woven, knitted and embroidered fabrics and trims. Many different types of job are available to textile designers within both fashion and textiles companies. Textile design is required for clothing and accessories; homeware; furniture upholstery and interiors; automotive and aeronautical industries, and this chapter concentrates primarily on textiles for fashion. A large proportion of textile designers work for fabric manufacturers, but many also work for suppliers or retailers of fashion or homeware products. Within the fashion industry textile designers usually remain anonymous to the consumer, with fashion designers taking the credit for the total design of the garments, using numerous sources of fabric which may have been designed by several textile designers working for various companies.

Some directional ready-to-wear designers incorporate print design as a key component of their signature look, viewing the relationship between garment and print as equally important, rather than print being subservient to the cut. Jonathan Saunders and Eley Kishimoto (see Chapter 4), who show their ranges on the runway at London Fashion Week, design their own original, exclusive prints. Textile designers are less feted than their fashion designing counterparts (somewhat unfairly) and tend not to be well-known to the general public. A rare exception to this rule is the renowned print designer Celia Birtwell who was famed for her abstract prints in the 1960s, often used in her fashion designer husband Ossie Clark's collections. She has recently undergone a revival in the fashion world, having been commissioned to design a range of prints for Topshop in 2005. Those who gain fame in textile design often specialise in interiors, as their names may become synonymous with the brands under which their designs are sold, such as Sue Timney of the design duo Timney Fowler.

WOVEN TEXTILE DESIGN

Designers of woven textiles often work for fabric mills, either on a permanent or freelance basis (see Chapter 17). They may also be employed by companies which manufacture tailored garments, as much of the design of these products is based on the development of woven fabrics, with limited changes to garment styling each season. As well as creative and transferable skills, attention to detail is essential when designing woven fabrics, to make sure that the design is technically correct. The main responsibilities of a woven fabric designer can include:

- selecting yarns for fabrics;
- designing the construction and colour of fabrics;
- liaising with customers such as garment suppliers or retailers;
- developing designs requested by customers;
- visiting trade fairs.

Woven cloth is produced on looms, with 'end' yarns running horizontally across the weft and 'picks' running vertically along the warp, parallel to the selvedge. The weight of the fabric is measured in grams per square metre and is affected by the size and fibre content of the yarn from which it is constructed. A designer working for a fabric mill is required to design the types of cloth in which the company specialises. Popular woven fabric constructions include:

- plain weave;
- twill;
- satin (warp-faced, shiny face and dull reverse);
- crepe.

Velvet and corduroy are examples of woven 'pile' fabrics which have a raised, soft surface. Jacquard, brocade and damask fabrics have a self-coloured pattern incorporated within the weave. Trade fairs which exhibit woven fabrics include *Première Vision* (PV) in Paris and *Interstoff* in Frankfurt. It is also relevant for designers of men's tailoring fabrics to visit the *Pitti Uomo* menswear show in Florence for inspiration.

Computer-aided design (CAD) is frequently used for woven fabric design as the cloth can easily be represented on the computer screen and colours can be applied quickly and effectively to the designs. Some woollen mills remain in the UK, mostly based in West Yorkshire, but as the vast majority of fabrics are manufactured overseas, students need to be realistic about the number of job vacancies in woven design that are available in this country. Graduates who have studied woven textiles may need to be prepared to branch out into another part of the industry such as sales or a more technical role.

KNITTED TEXTILE DESIGN

Designers of knitted textiles have usually studied knit within either a fashion or textiles-related degree. Most knitted fabrics are made with a weft-knit construction on circular knitting machines in 'courses' (horizontal rows of loops) and 'wales' (vertical columns of loops) and are popular for making underwear, nightwear and casual clothing. Standard knitted fabric constructions include:

- single jersey;
- interlock;
- rib;
- pointelle;
- fleece.

Knitted fabrics such as these are cut into pieces from which garments are sewn together and the resulting products are known as jerseywear. So-called 'true' knitwear consists mainly of jumpers and cardigans and is made directly from yarn knitted into the shapes from which the items are made. Knitwear designers usually develop ideas for the knit construction, pattern and garment design of knitted clothing and they can be employed by knitwear manufacturers, fashion retailers, yarn spinners and fashion forecasting companies (see Chapter 3). They have a strong affinity with textile designers due to their involvement with the selection of yarn, fabric construction and pattern (see Chapter 4).

Some design studios specialise in knitted textiles. Nixe Design is an example of a knitwear design studio which employs a team of full-time in-house designers and freelance designers, similar to the way in which print design studios operate (see below). The company offers customers advice on knitting yarns and techniques, but is not involved in garment manufacture. Swatches are produced on domestic knitting machines using yarn from UK and Italian spinners which are then sold to clients. They also exhibit at international trade shows. The design team begin working on trends more than a year ahead of the season, inspired by fashion forecasting packages, travelling and shopping for vintage garments. Nixe Design's sales executive Ben Fleming explains:

> We sell knitwear design ideas to customers including high street retailers in the UK and USA and designer brands such as Gucci. They buy the designs and the copyright and they can use them in the same way or purely for design inspiration. We are commissioned by our customers to produce design ideas, colour palettes and trend predictions.

PRINTED TEXTILE DESIGN

Printed textile designers develop design ideas suitable for printing onto woven or knitted fabric and it is beneficial for them to have an understanding of the methods by which the fabrics are manufactured and printed. They often specialise in certain areas of design such as menswear, womenswear or childrenswear, and they may become known for a particular style such as floral or abstract prints. The subject of printed textile design may also be described as surface pattern or surface decoration, as its implementation has much in common with the design of patterns which are applied to products other than fabric, particularly homeware and giftware. Printed textile designers can be employed by:

- fabric manufacturers;
- fabric printers;
- fabric converters;
- print design studios;
- fashion forecasting companies (see Chapter 3);
- garment suppliers;
- interiors or fashion brands;
- fashion retailers.

They may also work freelance for a number of clients from any of the categories above and it is advisable to gain experience within at least one of these areas of the industry before embarking on a freelance career (see Chapter 17).

Fabric manufacturers, printers and converters

Fabric printing can take place at the mill where fabric is manufactured or at a specialist fabric printing company, both of which require permanent or freelance print designers. Ranges of print ideas which can be applied to fabric in production are put together approximately a year ahead of the season by the printer's design team. Initially, the designs are usually printed in short runs, cut into squares and attached to small hangers (usually called 'headers') for easy storage, which the fabric company's sales representatives or agents show to garment manufacturers and retailers (see Chapter 8).

Most mass-produced fabrics are now printed using rotary screen-printing. Ink is pumped from inside the rotary screen as it is rolled over the top of the fabric and the pattern is repeated with each full turn of the roller. A separate screen is made for each individual colour within the design, so the more colours that are included in a print, the more expensive it will be to produce, due to the costs incurred in making screens and the extra time involved in the printing process. A more traditional method of applying pattern to fabrics is screen-printing by forcing ink through the holes on the screen with a squeegee, either manually or mechanically. In transfer printing, the print is applied onto paper and transferred onto synthetic fabrics by a machine through a combination of heat and pressure. Because each of these methods involves the repetition of a pattern, designers who work for printers must produce designs 'in repeat' to make them suitable for the printing process. Print designers can be involved in overseeing 'strike-offs' which are first samples of prints on the correct cloth prior to bulk production.

Converters are fabric suppliers who do not make their own fabrics. They provide a service by supplying fabric to order for garment manufacturers or fashion retailers, and they may employ their own print designers. Converters usually buy greige cloth from fabric mills and commission other companies to dye, print or finish it. This makes them very flexible as they can use different suppliers, possibly in more than one country, to respond effectively to changes in fashion.

Print design studios

A print design studio normally employs a team of designers to develop print ideas. Print studios can be owned by individuals but some grow out of partnerships of two or more print designers who prefer the communal aspect of working in a studio, rather than in isolation, and the more practical financial aspects of sharing facilities such as CAD, printing, scanning and copying equipment. The design team can include print and embroidery designers permanently employed in the studio as well as freelancers who work there temporarily on specific design briefs. Some studios also employ designers of woven or knitted fabric. A print design studio may service a wide range of market levels. For example, Baxter Fawcett design studio, based in London, sells to a variety of UK high street fashion retailers, including Monsoon and Debenhams as well as American designer brands Liz Claiborne and Ralph Lauren. Many UK-based design studios sell their prints in New York and Tokyo, often through agents based in these locations. The print designs may be bought directly by the retailers' or brands' buying departments or through their suppliers. Sample lengths of designs can be printed onto fabric and made into garments to present to clients. Many print design studios show ranges at *Indigo*, a trade show for fashion prints held at the same time as the fabric show PV in Paris. Other similar events are held in various cities worldwide.

The studio manager normally has less design work than the rest of the team and is responsible for managing the business by:

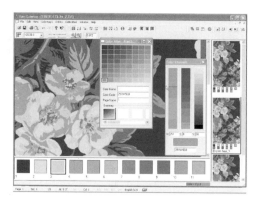

Fig. 2.2 Gerber Easy Coloring software
Courtesy of Gerber Technology

- liaising with clients and seeking new business;
- initiating new collections;
- co-ordinating the team's workload and allocating tasks to appropriate members of staff;
- approving strike-offs from fabric mills.

An experienced print designer within a studio develops ranges of print ideas and may also:

- liaise with clients on the direction and development of the designs;
- select appropriate trends and research for inspiration to meet a client's brief;
- visit trade fairs to investigate print and fabric trends or to sell designs.

Studio assistants work on design ideas for production which have been developed by experienced designers within the studio and may have the following responsibilities:

- recolouring prints by painting or using CAD software (see Fig. 2.2);
- putting designs into repeat;
- creating finished artwork;
- compiling storyboards;
- liaising with clients;
- buying art materials.

Garment suppliers

Some large garment suppliers offer their customers a print design service by employing print designers to work within the design team, either on a permanent or freelance basis. They develop all-over or placement print ideas to complement garment ranges in order to offer retailers a complete package of printed garment designs. Print designers who work for garment suppliers sometimes accompany fashion designers to meetings with fashion buyers to discuss the development of print ideas and may liaise with fabric suppliers or printers. The print designer is usually briefed by the supplier's head of design or by the retailer. Within garment suppliers, print designers often work on CAD systems to recolour prints or to 'drape' them onto fashion drawings produced by other members of the team.

Interiors or fashion brands and retailers

When working for brands or retailers, print designers work closely with fashion designers to develop garment ranges suitable for their target customers. Fashion retailers can also work directly with individual freelance print designers or print design studios to commission print designs or to purchase prints from existing artwork through meetings at the retailer's head office, the designer's studio or at a trade fair such as *Indigo*. Some furnishing and interiors brands employ colourists who do not design products or prints but develop colour stories for the product range, selecting colourways for specific plain or printed items to co-ordinate collections.

Computer-aided design (CAD)

Print designers can render their own designs by hand, with paint and various other media or use CAD programs, which are particularly appropriate for adding colour to designs. When designing with a CAD system it is usual to generate ideas by hand which can be scanned into the computer. A mouse or graphics tablet with a virtual pen connected to the computer can then be used to manipulate and colour prints. Adobe Illustrator® and Photoshop® are popular programs used by designers in various fields and several companies publish software specifically for print design (see Fig. 2.2). One of the advantages of developing designs on CAD systems is that they can be linked directly to large-scale digital printers and applied to fabrics for short runs and prototype garments. A CAD technique called texture mapping allows 2D designs to achieve a 3D effect by 'wrapping' them onto products such as garments or curtains to visualise the finished product.

EMBROIDERY DESIGN

Embroidery designers develop decorative stitching designs to be applied to fabrics and garments. In common with print design, an embroidered pattern can be an all-over which is in repeat, a border design on the edge of the fabric only or a placement design which is applied to a specific position on a garment. Embroidery can be applied by hand or by industrial embroidery machines. Hand embroidery has been a significant feature of women's fashion in recent years, often from India or the Far East. Much of the embroidery used in the production of garments is carried out by multi-head electronic embroidery machines and the designs can be stored in files on disks. Embroidery designers require awareness of the technical ability of the machinery which will be used to produce their designs, specifically the types of stitches that are available and threads that the machines can handle. It is possible to manipulate fabrics to create three-dimensional designs using beading, appliqué, pleating and quilting techniques. Embroidery designers mostly work in:

- specialist embroidery companies;
- textile design studios;
- costume design for film, TV or theatre;
- lingerie manufacturers or retailers;
- bridalwear companies.

DESIGNER/MAKERS

Textile designer/makers are craftspeople who produce limited edition or one-off fabrics or products such as accessories or artwork and are usually self-employed (see Chapter 17). The commercial outlets for these items can be exhibitions in galleries, craft fairs, design studios/workshops, craft retailers or websites. Designer/makers may have studied any branch of textile design or another art and design subject. They have a great amount of scope for creative freedom within their work, uninhibited by the limitations of working for suppliers or retailers, although this must be balanced with a certain degree of business awareness and commerciality if the business is intended to be financially viable. If so, the products must appeal to potential customers and sell at a profit. The designer/maker requires a studio or workshop with suitable facilities or can work from home. The materials within the products may not be inherently expensive but the investment in costs such as premises and other resources, as well as the time spent designing and creating them have to be reflected in the products' selling prices, making them relatively expensive in comparison to mass-produced items. The Crafts Council offers services and sources of funding to designer/makers and houses an exhibition gallery and shop at its London headquarters.

FIBRE CONTENT OF FABRICS

Textile designers can design fabrics made from a variety of different fibres. Selecting the fibre content of the fabric can be part of the design process, so it is useful for textile designers to be aware of the different fibres which are available and their properties. Fabrics can be made from either natural or synthetic (man-made) fibres such as the following:

Plant fibres

- cotton;
- linen;

- ramie;
- bamboo.

Animal fibres

- wool;
- silk;
- alpaca;
- mohair;
- angora.

Synthetic fibres

- nylon (polyamide);
- polyester;
- acrylic;
- acetate;
- viscose.

Synthetic fibres are manufactured from various raw materials using chemical processes. Nylon, for example, is made from petroleum by-products and the main raw material for viscose is wood pulp. Yarn producers buy fibres and spin them into different types and counts (sizes) of yarn. Fibre content can be identified by details in care labels which are legally required in garments sold in the UK.

FABRIC CONSTRUCTION

Fabric manufacturers weave or knit yarns to make fabrics. Textile designers are employed to design either the construction or the surface of fabrics, such as printing or embroidery. Fabric mills usually manufacture undyed fabric which they call 'greige goods' and this unfinished cloth can be coloured by printing or dyeing, or both. Alternatively, yarn can be dyed in advance to produce 'yarn-dyed' or 'colour-woven' fabrics to give a clear, crisp colour quality. Yarn-dyeing is a relatively expensive, time-consuming process as decisions on colour need to be made in advance and the yarns need to be dyed in the correct quantities and placed in the correct location for weaving. This is suitable for woven stripes or checks such as tartan or gingham as each colour follows the warp or weft of the cloth. Designers can select different-coloured yarns to produce yarn-dyed stripes for knitted fabrics. Fabrics have various properties which woven and knitted textile designers can incorporate in their designs, including aesthetic qualities such as lustre and pattern and functional aspects including strength, durability and elasticity. Innovative fabrics have also been developed with properties such as waterproofing or biodegradability (see Chapter 6).

CAREER ROUTES

A typical start to a career in textile design would be as an assistant designer within a design studio, fabric supplier, garment supplier, retailer or brand. With two years experience or more it is possible to become a textile designer. After several years of designing it is possible to become the manager of a team of designers. Textile designers can attract reasonable salaries which are often higher in large companies. Working freelance is a particularly popular option for textile designers as they can earn a more lucrative hourly rate than employees of a company but a steady stream of work from various clients is necessary to make this viable.

Numerous universities in the UK offer BA (Hons) Textiles Design and related courses including BA (Hons) Surface Decoration which incorporates print techniques applicable not just to fashion but also cards, gift wrapping, tiles and ceramics. Courses dealing with the construction of textiles may focus on either knitted or woven fabrics, some of which result in a BSc degree due to the depth of technical knowledge required. Students are offered the opportunity to specialise in embroidery within certain textile design degrees. Several universities offer degrees combining the study of fashion and textile design, enabling their graduates to progress into either of these fields, or to pursue careers encompassing both areas. Textile design graduates can also pursue careers in fashion buying (see Chapter 8), fabric technology (see Chapter 6) or fashion styling (see Chapter 15) as their knowledge of fabrics is advantageous in these roles.

CASE STUDIES

Print designer for a garment supplier

Career path

Anna Proctor is a textile and graphic designer at Castleblair plc, a manufacturer of womenswear for Marks & Spencer, where she describes her role as 'anything to do with print'. She took A levels including textiles before studying an art and design foundation course, followed by a BA (Hons) Printed Textile Design degree. Shortly after graduating in 2002, through a contact at university Anna became an assistant print designer at Addison Smith, a textile agency representing fabric mills. Anna worked there until being offered her current job in 2005.

Role and responsibilities

Anna is located in the design team of the company's London-based office alongside three fashion designers (see Fig. 2.3). She works with them on print-related concepts, including placement prints and embroideries. Anna explains:

> *Because my print designs are always developed within a garment shape, rather than purely artwork, my perspective on what a print does is different now. Print can be about balance of colour and how fabric drapes.*

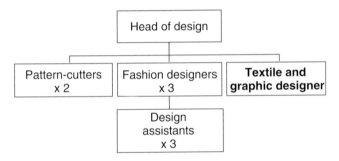

Fig. 2.3 Design department structure at Castleblair

Anna also works closely with Castleblair's fabric technologist on fabric development and sourcing. She finds inspiration for her designs from the mood boards presented by the Marks & Spencer design team, catwalk reports, and observing other fashion retailers. Anna designs using CAD programs to scan, manipulate and recolour print ideas. She makes initial presentations of design ideas for a garment range to the selectors (buyers) at Marks & Spencer about seven months before the merchandise is delivered to stores, so the ability to predict fashion trends is vital. Anna liaises with the retailer regularly and explains that she joins Castleblair's commercial director at weekly meetings at the Marks & Spencer head office 'so that it's not Chinese whispers about the designs and we can supply products more quickly'.

As part of her job, Anna goes on directional shopping trips to Paris and London with her colleagues to buy garments which she finds interesting or inspiring, as well as visiting PV. This sounds entertaining but Anna admits 'it is really tiring to spend an entire day scrutinising the shops'. She explains that she develops her own original print ideas:

Because European fabric mills (who offer their own print ranges) have now become too expensive to use and we can offer exclusive prints to Marks & Spencer which are not available elsewhere.

To source fabric, she travels to the Turkish mills which usually produce her prints, as Castleblair's garment production is based in Turkey. Anna says:

People have an idea that you can turn around exquisite designs quickly but it's not that simple. I was based in a Turkish fabric mill for two months in my first job to get a good understanding of how they work, so I know how to phrase things for them. Generally I let the fabric supplier put my designs into repeat. But once a mill didn't do this properly, leaving gaps in the print design, which caused problems with our deadline. So I've learnt that if it's essential for a print to be right first-time I have to put it into repeat myself.

Selectors can buy products based on seeing CAD designs, but some still like to receive sample garments before making the decision. When the Marks & Spencer selector is interested in buying a product featuring one of Anna's print designs Castleblair's commercial team calculate the costing for the garment and negotiate the cost price, quantities and delivery dates. When the order has been confirmed, the selector requests items such as strike-offs and Anna keeps in contact with the suppliers to make sure they are delivered to as high a standard as possible, within the required deadline. She prepares the print design for a strike-off with clear, detailed instructions for the Turkish mill, and sends new instructions if amendments to the strike-off are necessary. Anna usually works on more than one season at a time, e.g. following up the production of prints which have been selected by Marks & Spencer for autumn/winter whilst creating ideas for the next spring/summer range. Consequently, Anna says:

> *You need to be a brilliant multi-tasker to meet the deadlines in this type of job. You can work on something for months then be asked to change it within a week, so you are torn between what to do and when to do it.*

Though it is undoubtedly hard work, Anna describes what she enjoys most about her job:

> *I like drawing and painting and working with the customer, providing what they're looking for. It's very satisfying seeing it right through from beginning to end and you get a sense of having achieved something. It's great when you see someone walking down the street wearing one of your designs.*

Anna receives feedback about her designs from the selectors. She can occasionally be found lurking outside Marks & Spencer on Saturdays to see what type of customers are in the store and she says she has been known to 'subtly tail' people in the womenswear department to see which products they are interested in buying!

Career advice

When employing textiles graduates Anna looks for evidence of the following in interviewees:

- good organisational skills;
- good communication skills;
- market awareness;
- good sense of aesthetics and colour;
- confidence;
- no pretensions.

Anna rates self-motivation and organisation as the most important skills required in her job, with creativity and computer skills also being significant. Her advice to textiles graduates is for them to find out about the different employment options available to them. As a student, she didn't know that the type of job she now does existed and believed her only career options were as a studio designer or lecturer. Anna recommends students to find work experience during their courses. She did placements at *World of Interiors* magazine and an interior design company which helped her to realise she didn't want to work in this field.

Woven fabric designer for a design studio

Career path

Becky Hance is a textile designer at Palm Design in London, where she has worked since graduating with a BA (Hons) Textile Design degree specialising in woven textiles in 2002.

Role and responsibilities

Becky's position involves designing woven fabrics within a creative design team alongside a leading fabric supplier to the UK high street (see Fig. 2.4). The company is a design studio producing woven, knitted and printed textile designs for clients within the fashion and textiles industry. Becky's role is to develop innovative commercial designs for the menswear and womenswear woven fabric collections following the design process from initial idea and inspiration to final fabric production. Her role also includes the design and development of CAD and hand-produced designs for Palm Design's in-house studio collection, creating a range of stripes, checks and embellishments directed towards the European and American fashion market from designer collections to high street stores.

Becky concentrates on designing for one season at a time whilst collating visual inspiration for the following season. She constantly liaises with clients both in the UK and USA through daily discussions to identify her customers' needs and requirements. She recently had the opportunity to join the sales team in New York to liaise with one of her customers in person. Becky describes her favourite elements of the job as:

> The opportunity to work within a creative environment, designing on a daily basis and having the excuse to shop – for inspiration, of course!

She believes teamwork within the design studio is very important in order to develop a collection which provides a range of designs suitable for all of the studio's customers. She considers communication, self-motivation and creativity to be the most important skills required within her job, adding:

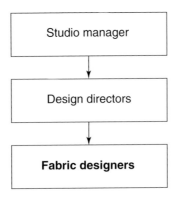

Fig. 2.4 Structure of the design team at Palm Design

Communication skills are essential in order for a design studio to be successful and run smoothly in such a demanding industry.

Career advice

Becky defines the main qualities her employer looks for when appointing textile designers as:

- a strong portfolio;
- market awareness;
- understanding of the latest fashion trends and the ability to interpret them through individual design work;
- a good team player with enthusiasm;
- a friendly personality.

She offers the following advice on finding a job as a woven textile designer:

Think of your portfolio as a working sketchbook, constantly adding to and improving it. Even if you are happy in your current position, you never know what opportunities may arise and it is essential to be prepared. Keep your portfolio as broad as possible to show a range of skills: the more experience and self-initiated projects included within the portfolio the more attractive you are to the employer.

FURTHER READING

Books

Anstey, H. and Weston, T. (1997) *The Anstey Weston Guide to Textile Terms.* Weston Publishing Limited, London.

Braddock, S. E. and O'Mahony, M. (2005) *Techno Textiles: Revolutionary Fabrics for Fashion and Design.* No. 2 Thames & Hudson, London.

Cresswell, L. (2002) *Textiles at the Cutting Edge.* Second edition. Forbes Publications, London.

Gale, C. and Kaur, J. (2002) *The Textile Book.* Berg, Oxford.

Magazines and journals

International Textiles
Textile View

Websites

www.craftscouncil.org.uk
www.gerbertechnology.com
www.premiere.vision.fr
texi.org

Fashion forecasting and illustration

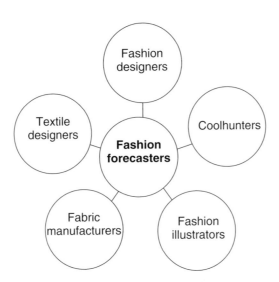

Fig. 3.1 Liaison between fashion forecasters and other roles

Fashion forecasting materials provide predictions of trends in colour, fabric and styling of fashion products for a particular season. These predictions are essential within the industry because most fashion merchandise needs to be designed well in advance of the season in which it will be sold to allow sufficient time for it to be developed, manufactured and delivered before eventually being available to consumers. Consequently, it is usual for fashion and textiles companies to begin the development of design concepts for each season's range a year or more ahead of its arrival in stores. Trend predictions cover general or specific areas of fashion and textiles, including:

- fabrics – woven or knitted, printed or plain;
- womenswear;

- menswear;
- childrenswear;
- knitwear;
- interiors.

Most designers and buyers use some form of fashion forecasting to enable them to predict key trends which they can adapt to the tastes of their target customers. The process of trend prediction can involve:

- visiting trade fairs;
- identification of trends in ready-to-wear collections;
- awareness of 'street' trends;
- compilation of colour palettes for themes;
- compilation of storyboards for themes;
- illustration of key looks.

Illustrators are briefed to develop images to visualise the trend concepts for fashion forecasting publications. Illustrators do not usually design the garments they draw but illustrate concepts developed by fashion designers. As well as trend predictions, fashion illustrators can work in a wide variety of other areas of the industry including fashion retail and the media.

FASHION FORECASTING PACKAGES

Fashion and textiles trend prediction packages are usually sold within the industry 18 months to a year ahead of the specified season. These packages usually take the form of a printed publication which can include colour palettes, yarns or fabrics, garment drawings, photographs and storyboards supported by relevant text. Some of the key trend prediction companies are:

- Nelly Rodi (Holland);
- Promostyl (France);
- Carlin International (France);
- Peclers (France);
- Trend Union (Holland);
- International Colour Authority (UK);
- wgsn.com (UK);
- Here and There (USA).

The International Colour Authority (ICA) was established in 1966 when trade publishers from Amsterdam, New York and London decided to collaborate in the compilation of trend predictions. The ICA is now based in London and continues to publish six-monthly forecasts of colour trends almost two years ahead of the season. Fashion forecasting company wgsn publishes its predictions online in addition to industry news, careers advice and a variety of fashion reports by subscription. Certain fashion forecasting companies focus on particular product areas, e.g. Concepts Paris, which specialises in lingerie. Fashion forecasting packages can be bought directly from the forecasting company, via sales agents in various countries or through specialist fashion publication retailers such as R.D. Franks in London.

Most fashion forecasting publications offer trend presentations by their representatives to customers as a service which may be inclusive in the price of the annual subscription. They are sometimes invited to present lectures to students on a particular season's trends, especially if the educational institution purchases the package. The company can also present trend information at fabric or garment trade fairs as a form of promotion to the industry. Fashion forecasting companies' design teams define trend concepts, deriving inspiration from a variety of contemporary and historical cultural elements: designer and street fashion; travel; music; films; TV and art. They can be commissioned to produce predictions by fashion retailers who may request colour palettes and styling ideas to be compiled to cater for their target markets. Colour palettes are shown in separate colour stories, usually incorporating pastel, mid and dark tones. A colour story can be combined with mood boards (or storyboards) showing visuals of colour inspiration, fabric swatches and styling influences, to create a theme which can influence the work of fashion and textile designers in the companies which subscribe to the fashion forecasting packages.

Fashion forecasting magazines

International Textiles and *Textile View* are bi-monthly magazines concentrating on fabric predictions for future seasons. A more economical option than fashion forecasting packages, they also feature garment styling predictions six months to a year ahead of the season (see Fig. 3.2). *Viewpoint* is a sister publication to *Textile View*, containing mainly lifestyle-orientated trends which impact upon the fashion market. Weekly fashion industry journal *Drapers* often features fabric and fashion predictions commissioned from fashion forecasting companies in relation to yarn and fabric trade fairs.

Sources of fashion predictions

The first stage in fashion forecasting is the compilation of colour palettes created by panels of fashion and interiors colour specialists from around the world. The British Textile Colour Group (BTCG) is a body of fabric and fashion design consultants and colourists who meet twice a year to devise colour palettes two years ahead of the season. Members of the BTCG debate the direction in which colours are likely to develop, bringing swatches, yarns, photographs and materials in relevant shades to enable them to make joint decisions on a season's definitive colour stories. Other countries also have their own panels which compile colour predictions such as the French *Comité Français de la Couleur* and the Color Marketing

Fig. 3.2 Fashion forecasting illustration from International Textiles for spring/summer 2007 Courtesy of International Textiles

Group in the USA. Many participants in these colour forecasting groups are involved in devising colour palettes for fabric and yarn trade fairs. Representatives of colour forecasting panels from various countries contribute to a global trend organisation known as Intercolour. Fabric and garment predictions are largely inspired by a combination of influences which initially appear to be at opposite ends of the spectrum: directional ready-to-wear designers and street fashion. Coolhunters are employed by fashion forecasting companies to seek out global influences on future trends by identifying individuals and groups within subcultures who have developed innovative styles of clothing. Colour, fabric and styling predictions originated by these methods filter down to fashion designers working for fashion retailers and suppliers to the high street, which accounts for the frequent similarities between colours and styling between products in competing stores.

Yarn predictions

Colour predictions for knitting yarns are forecast further ahead than other areas of the industry because the yarn production process has a longer timescale than that of fabric. Consequently, yarn predictions are issued by fashion forecasting companies earlier than any other product area and yarn shows *Pitti Filati* and *Expofil* take place ahead of fabric and fashion trade fairs. Specialist knitwear prediction studios are often involved in the development of yarn types and knitted swatches to promote yarn suppliers' products in packages issued to customers and for visual presentations at yarn fairs.

FASHION ILLUSTRATION

Fashion illustrators work mostly on a freelance basis (see Chapter 17) providing illustrations when required by the following types of business amongst others:

- magazines;
- newspapers;
- books;
- fashion forecasting companies;
- fashion websites;
- fashion designers;
- fashion retailers;
- fashion brands.

An illustrator may be employed regularly by a company, particularly if the illustrative style becomes strongly associated with the publication or brand by consumers. The items to be illustrated are provided in the form of products or photographs from which the illustrator can draw. Fashion illustrators may also exhibit their work through art dealers or galleries, either individually or jointly selling their artwork to the public. Fashion designers at all market levels develop their ideas through drawing and some use fashion illustrations to communicate their ideas to colleagues and customers within the trade.

Fashion illustration within the press

Fashion magazines and newspapers offer some of the best opportunities for regular illustration commissions. Most daily newspapers have fashion pages on a weekly basis and Sunday newspapers have fashion sections in colour magazines which can contain illustrated articles. Fashion illustration in the press suffered a demise after the 1950s due to the domination of photography but has undergone a renaissance since the 1990s, fuelled by publications which have exposed a diversity of styles and techniques and the development of CAD programs.

Fashion illustration for designers, brands or retailers

Fashion designers, brands or retailers can brief illustrators to draw their products for advertising, product labelling, packaging and in-store promotional material including posters, brochures, postcards and storecards. Fashion illustrators have become more widely recognised for their creative influence on fashion in recent years and the appointment of illustrator Julie Verhoeven as the designer for Italian ready-to-wear manufacturer Gibo in 2003 gained high-profile publicity. Having previously worked as an assistant to both John Galliano and Martine Sitbon and having collaborated with Louis Vuitton and Cacharel gave her the advantage of seeing how designers operate at this level. Jeffrey Fulvimari was already a popular fashion illustrator when he was asked to illustrate Madonna's children's book *The English Roses* in 2003. Since then his 'Bobbypin' brand has been licensed in the UK for a wide variety of fashion products and his illustrations have been featured on womenswear styles in New Look in 2004 and childrenswear in Marks & Spencer in 2005. Fashion illustrators are not limited to commissions within the fashion industry and their clients are often in search of a fashionable look to be applied to a variety of other products.

Illustration media and CAD

Illustrators have their own 'handwriting' based on their definitive use of media, line, composition and content, which gives their work a recognisable style. There has been a strong trend for CAD illustration since the development of vector-based programs Adobe Illustrator® and CorelDRAW® which produce smooth lines, the most famous practitioner of this style being Jason Brooks who has produced illustrations for *Vogue*, *Elle* and fashion retailer Oasis. The use of collage and photography within illustrations became fashionable during the 1990s, often in conjunction with CAD. Other illustrators still favour traditional media like ink or oil paint.

PAYMENT FOR FASHION ILLUSTRATION

As fashion illustrators are invariably freelance, they need to make decisions about remuneration for their work. Payment is usually per illustration, rather than charging an hourly rate. The illustrator should consider the time the work will take, however, to make the price viable, including research, preparation and the development of ideas. Illustrators often receive commissions for their work through agents who introduce them to clients. In order to calculate a realistic and profitable fashion illustration fee the following factors should be considered:

- the end use of the illustration;
- the geographical area of use;
- duration of use by the client;
- the client's profile and budget;
- the illustrator's reputation;
- contribution towards materials, equipment, premises and bills;
- expenses for travel and postage incurred in the commission;
- commission paid to an agent;
- the time factor.

The Association of Illustrators (theaoi.com) provides detailed advice on charges for illustrations.

CAREER ROUTES

There are no definitive career routes within fashion forecasting and illustration as so many who work in these fields are self-employed freelancers or consultants. A limited number of companies in fashion forecasting are large enough to offer a promotional structure in which junior and senior design positions may be offered in menswear, womenswear or childrenswear. As a fashion forecaster or illustrator gains experience, receives wider coverage and builds up a reputation within the business it is possible to charge higher fees. People who work in fashion forecasting are frequently graduates in fashion or textile design. Some illustrators have a degree related to fashion or textiles but many have studied illustration or graphics. BA (Hons) Fashion Promotion and Illustration at Surrey Institute is the most well-known course in the UK focusing specifically on this subject.

CASE STUDIES

Freelance fashion illustrator

Career path

David Downton is a fashion illustrator who has worked for numerous clients including *The Times, The Independent, The Daily Telegraph, Visionaire, Vogue,* Barneys of New York, Harvey Nichols and Estée Lauder (see Fig. 3.3). He graduated in

Fig. 3.3 Fashion illustrator David Downton in his studio
Courtesy of David Downton

1981 with BA(Hons) Graphics and Illustration, with 'no ambition except to be able to draw every day'. During his course he studied life drawing and admired the work of the great fashion illustrators Eric, Antonio and Gruau (whom he describes as a 'graphic genius'). He began a successful career as a commercial illustrator for a variety of different products from CD covers to wine labels and menus, as well as the occasional fashion illustration for which his loose, figurative style was particularly appropriate. In 1996 David started to focus mainly on fashion after being briefed by the *Financial Times* to illustrate a feature on the couture shows in Paris.

Role and responsibilities

David's work mainly involves doing fashion illustrations in his studio as well as:

- attending fashion shows;
- exhibiting his work;
- portrait painting;
- meetings with clients.

David can be working on between two to six projects at once. The computer in his studio is used only for emailing as he never uses CAD in his work. He sums up the process he follows to produce his definitive drawing style:

I draw on layout paper using pen or graphite and keep drawing. I don't always draw every part of the body, but I know where they all are. I want it to make sense, to explain how the arm works. I do 10–20 drawings and take what's right from each one. I then work on a light-box on A2 size or larger and I try to create the illusion that the drawing was effortless. I want it to look like I tipped over the ink and it fell into place while I was out of the room. I'm addicted to black Rotring ink. I also use gouache, watercolour, crayon, pastels and oilsticks. For flat colour I use a coloured background and overlay acetate on it.

David is constantly inspired by the Paris couture shows and he has been back there every season since 1996:

It's not about the shows, it's the whole package. It's a fantasy world and the clothes are made with love – they're like works of art that might have been created by 50 people. When I first saw Erin O'Connor at a Gaultier show my mouth dropped open because she was like a living representation of the figure that I draw. This coincided with my first exhibition in London so I contacted her agent and invited him to see it. I have an ongoing collaboration with her and I'll never tire of it.

During the runway shows he takes photographs as an *aide-memoire* and draws the models afterwards, sometimes within half-an-hour during garment fittings. David has agents in London and New York who negotiate with clients and charge a percentage of the final fee for this service and his work is also promoted on illustration websites. He has had a constant stream of work throughout his career and

Fig. 3.4 Illustration by David Downton
Courtesy of David Downton

though in the past this occasionally involved accepting jobs he wasn't keen on, he is now in the fortunate position of choosing which projects he wants to pursue. His recent commissions include illustrations for the Ritz Carlton hotel in Miami and milliner Phillip Treacy's hotel in Ireland. David's clients brief him either on the phone or in meetings, which may consist of several people in a boardroom. He can also be briefed via an intermediary such as one of his agents.

David has exhibited his illustrations in three one-man shows in London and one in New York in 2002. His first portrait was of model Marie Helvin after he met her at one of his exhibitions, and he has subsequently drawn many more including Catherine Deneuve, Stella Tennant and Iman. During his meetings with sitters he draws them in his sketchbook and later completes the portraits in his studio (see Fig. 3.4). As well as the glamorous aspects of his job he has to carry out more mundane tasks like scanning images and driving to the Post Office. When asked what he likes best about his job he replies:

Almost everything about it. I make my living by the thing that I'm best at, which is a privilege, but there's a lot of pressure to perform and to meet deadlines, with no time to pause and reflect. People always expect the best of you.

Career advice

David offers the following advice for would-be fashion illustrators:

> *You've got to be ready for work and fairly confident of your own talent as there can be lots of knock-backs. You have to be available, keen and not be put off. You need to be very aware of your market, which is anything you want it to be, oil painting or Mac design – there's enough work to go round. Look at what you think are the 10 best magazines and decide which ones you want to be in. Have the fantasy in your head of what your ideal job would be. Go and see people and spend money on putting together a professional-looking portfolio. It doesn't need to be huge in size or number of pieces but should represent the best of you and it should be as good as it can be at that point. Be persistent and ring people where you see your work fitting in. You need tenacity and social skills to be able to talk to people. I didn't know any of the people in the fashion business and I had to learn very fast, talking on the phone and being able to interpret ideas. Clients remember you as well as your work.*

FURTHER READING

Books

Borelli, L. (2000) *Fashion Illustration Now.* Thames & Hudson, London.
Borelli, L. (2003) *Fashion Illustration Next.* Thames & Hudson, London.
Dawber, M. (2004) *Imagemakers: Cutting Edge Fashion Illustration.* Mitchell Beazley, London.
Dawber, M. (2005) *New Fashion Illustration.* Batsford, London.
McKelvey, K. and Munslow, M. (1997) *Illustrating Fashion.* Blackwell Publishing, Oxford.

Magazines

Drapers
International Textiles
Textile View
Viewpoint

Websites

www.internationalcolorauthority.com
www.itbd.co.uk
www.theaoi.com
www.view-publications.com
www.wgsn.com

Fashion design 4

Fig. 4.1 Liaison between fashion designers and other job roles

This chapter aims to show the breadth of job opportunities that are available within fashion design. The fashion designer's role is to design appropriate products for a specific target market, price bracket and season. Jobs in fashion design can vary greatly in terms of the market at which the designs are aimed, i.e. the price, type of customer and retail outlet. There are many different types of fashion merchandise and the designer is likely to concentrate on a particular product area. Fashion designers can work for suppliers, retailers, ready-to-wear labels or brands. Ready-to-wear designers have arguably the most coveted jobs in the fashion industry. Many of these designers, either working in the UK or internationally, have studied renowned courses which help to give British fashion design graduates an enviable and prestigious reputation throughout the world.

WHAT DO FASHION DESIGNERS DO?

Fashion designers usually specialise in menswear, womenswear or childrenswear. Within each category they usually target a particular age range or customer lifestyle, such as menswear aimed at 25–40 year olds. Some fashion designers are responsible for several different product types, particularly if they work in small companies or at a senior level in a large business. Designers can specialise in specific product types such as:

- tailoring;
- casualwear;
- sportswear;
- knitwear;
- jerseywear;
- lingerie and underwear;
- swimwear;
- occasionwear;
- clubwear;
- eveningwear;
- nightwear.

Sometimes the job is narrowly focused on individual garment types, e.g. women's jackets in very large companies, such as suppliers to Marks & Spencer, which sell styles in sizeable quantities. It can be useful for the designer to gain detailed experience but some designers may feel restricted within a limited product area. In addition to garments, accessories are significant fashion items and designers are also required for millinery and footwear.

Fashion designers have several different responsibilities. In whichever area of the market they work, most fashion designers' jobs comprise the following tasks:

- trend research;
- directional and comparative shopping;
- sourcing fabric and trims;
- design;
- range presentations;
- development meetings.

Depending on the company they work for, fashion designers may also:

- compile design specifications;
- cut patterns (see Chapter 5);

- fit garments (see Chapter 7);
- prepare garments for fashion shows.

Trend research

Fashion designers need to forecast fashion trends because the process of design, development and production usually takes several months and this timescale can be lengthened if goods are imported from a long distance (see Chapter 3). The move towards so-called 'fast fashion' within many retailers means that the design-ers have a much shorter product development period so that the store can respond to new trends within a matter of weeks. Trend research is compiled from of a variety of information which can include:

- sketches of garments seen in shops or magazines (usually from designer level);
- 'tear sheets' (pages of relevant products from magazines);
- fashion websites;
- fabric swatches;
- trade fairs;
- fashion forecasting packages.

Designers who work for retailers give presentations to their buying colleagues and sometimes to the design teams of their suppliers to ensure they work on the same key themes. Designers who work for suppliers also give trend presentations to retail buyers. Designers compile storyboards which usually take the form of a professionally-presented collage, filled mainly with photographs from current fashion magazines, featuring the main trends for the retailer for the particular season. Titles are selected for each theme as well as colour palettes, swatches of key fabrics, prints, garments and styling details. Fashion retailers usually produce colour palettes for each season or selling phase to distribute amongst their fabric and garment suppliers, to match colours and prints for mass production to ensure that products made by different companies in various countries co-ordinate effec-tively (Goworek 2001).

Trade fairs

Fashion and fabric trade fairs focusing on specific areas of the market usually take place twice a year. The fabric trade fair *Première Vision* (PV) is a very popular destination for designers and buyers, used as the starting point for the dev-elopment of many retailers or suppliers' garment ranges for the following spring/summer or autumn/winter, and is often combined with a directional shopping trip. Various fashion trade fairs are available for different market sectors, aimed at a range of product types, age groups, lifestyles and price brackets, in-cluding *Mode Enfantine* and *La Salon de la Lingerie* in Paris and *Pure Womenswear* in London (see Chapter 8). Trade fairs are accessible to people in the fashion business, such as buyers, designers and sales agents, and some admit students, but it is advisable to book tickets in advance. Lists of trade fairs are published regularly in *Drapers*.

Directional shopping

Directional shopping refers to trips to gain design inspiration for a new season. Depending on the product type and the company's travel budget, designers visit major fashion cities, sometimes accompanied by colleagues from design and buying teams.

Fashion designers visit the stores of the most influential designers and retailers, usually in a higher price bracket than the market they design for, and return armed with notes, sketches and garments for inspiration (referred to as 'bought samples'). London, Paris and New York are destinations popular with designers for most product types and market levels. Milan is often visited by lingerie designers whilst childrenswear designers may find more inspiration in Tokyo. In London designers usually aim for the major fashion department stores Harrods, Harvey Nichols and Selfridges as well as designer stores and boutiques in areas such as Bond Street and Notting Hill Gate. In Paris the main department stores which stock designer fashion are *Galeries Lafayette* and *Au Printemps*, with many designer stores located on the Left Bank. A directional shopping trip to New York usually includes visits to Macy's, Bloomingdales and Henri Bendel in Manhattan. In Milan *La Rinascente* is the key department store in the centre of the city within walking distance of the exclusive shopping area in the vicinity of *Via della Spiga* and *Via Montenapoleone.*

Though such trips sound glamorous and are undoubtedly interesting and useful, they can be tiring as designers represent the company day and night for the duration of the visit, working long hours to maximise the available time and often socialising afterwards with colleagues, clients and suppliers. Consecutive trips to different cities may be organised and it is usually expected that designers will be available to travel during weekends when required.

Comparative shopping

Comparative shopping, often called a 'comp. shop' in the trade, is usually carried out by designers several times per season. This involves observing ranges in competing stores which sell comparable products at similar prices. Reports are occasionally produced after a comp. shop visit, to be shared with other members of design and buying teams (see Chapter 9). Information is noted about the products, prices, fabrics and colourways of competitors' merchandise and sketches or photographs may be added. The aim of a comp. shop is not usually to copy competing retailers' products but to be aware of the choice of merchandise on offer to the target customer to ensure that the company that the designer works for offers the consumer value for money and is aware of developments.

Sourcing fabrics and trims

Fabric sourcing involves the selection of fabrics for sampling and bulk production of garments. Fabric sourcing is an essential part of the creative process as it is necessary to select the fabrics from which a product range can be made. Fabric choice plays a substantial part in the aesthetics and performance of a fashion designer's garment ideas. Fashion buyers and fabric technologists often participate in fabric sourcing (see Chapter 6) either in conjunction with designers or by pre-selecting fabrics which they consider to be appropriate for the target market. Details of the price per metre, width, washability and delivery timescale are required for the designer to be aware of a fabric's suitability for the customer. If the fabric fits these criteria and is considered to have the right aesthetic appeal, the designer requests a hanger of fabric which can be used for reference. A sample length of fabric can be requested to make up a sample garment. Designers also source other materials, trims and components including interlinings, fastenings and braid using similar methods. It is customary for designers to select fabric and trims before designing to provide them with visual and tactile inspiration for their ideas.

Fabric knowledge

Fabric knowledge is very beneficial to designers when sourcing and designing and this is mostly picked up through experience, though it is an advantage to have learnt about textiles during a degree course (see Chapter 2). Fabrics can be of knitted or woven construction and it is important for fashion designers to have an awareness of properties such as stretch, texture and drape of the fabrics with which they are designing, as these factors directly affect the fit and appearance of garments. Designers become familiar with the aspects of the fabrics they use regularly and can maximise their effect when designing garments. The fashion designer is also responsible for developing ideas for the colourways of plain and printed fabric to be used in a particular garment design, often in liaison with a print designer. If the fabric is to be printed or embroidered the fashion designer may select a print from a fabric manufacturer or print studio, or brief a textile designer to design the required type of pattern.

Design

When designing it is essential to take into account the lifestyle of the potential customer at whom the range is aimed. Fashion designers create ideas and make decisions in relation to:

- silhouette;
- design detail;
- fabric;
- colour;
- pattern;
- trims and fastenings.

Design development

Designers draw numerous initial design concepts before developing those with the most commercial potential. Variations on the most successful design ideas are sketched to view a series of potential alternatives. Once a designer has chosen a suitable silhouette for a jacket, for example, different collar shapes, pockets and seams can be applied to the design before arriving at the definitive version. Fashion designers apply elements of the trends they have researched to products suitable for the target market. Designers may make their own decisions about which direction the designs should take or they may consult a senior designer to seek advice on the commerciality of their concepts. Whichever area of the market they cater for, fashion designers have to work within certain parameters when designing, such as:

- the customer's aesthetic tastes;
- the retailer's price range;
- the technical performance of the fabric and the completed garment.

The extent of the designer's creativity is constrained within these parameters to enable a commercial solution to a design brief to be found, whether the product forms part of a luxury designer collection or a value-led mass market range. Other factors may be important in the design philosophy for certain companies and there is an increasing interest in ethical and environmental concerns within fashion and textiles, as the industry consumes enormous amounts of resources globally. Recycled fabric became fashionable in the 1990s through UK designer labels Fake London and Jessica Ogden's garments made from recycled textiles and clothing. Appealing to contemporary consumer issues, some brands use organic fibres within their product ranges and a 'green' stance can also be adopted by mass market companies within Fair Trade and Eco policies.

Many designers try to stretch the boundaries in which their creative skills are confined, a quality which is often considered to go hand-in-hand with a creative personality. With support from technical colleagues this can encourage innovation within the company's product range, to ensure that the business continues to progress. Fashion designers frequently receive criticism within the industry for lacking technical skills and concentrating too much on drawing. Designers who can consistently produce innovative concepts within technical and financial limits are viewed as valuable assets to the fashion industry.

Graphic design for clothing

With the long-term popularity of placement prints within all areas of fashion over the last decade, many companies require designers to produce graphic images for their clothing. This may be part of the fashion designer's job for a small company but within a large business an individual designer may concentrate on this area. Technical knowledge of garment construction is not vital in this job therefore graduates in textiles or graphics often work in this type of role.

Fashion drawing techniques

Fashion designers use a variety of drawing styles for different purposes and each person has his or her own personal variation on these techniques (see Chapter 3). Most fashion drawings fall into one of the following categories:

- sketches (also known as 'roughs') for initial design development ideas;
- working drawings (also called flats or schematic drawings) for spec. sheets or for presenting selected design ideas;
- fashion illustrations for presenting design ideas.

Design ideas may sometimes be developed in sketchbooks, but usually to speed up the process many professional fashion designers use sheets of printer paper or layout paper. Within a working environment, these sketches are often seen only by the designer, so it is not vital for them to be overly detailed and precise. Sketches are a visible representation of the thought process behind fashion design. Working drawings need to be clear and sharp as they are invariably used to communicate information about the design to other people. The test of a good working drawing is that it can be interpreted accurately by another designer or a pattern cutter in the way the original designer intended (see Fig. 4.2). If they are being used to show a range of ideas to a buyer, they may also have fabric swatches attached and colour added to them with various media such as Pantone® fibre-tip pens or CAD programs.

CAD programs such as Adobe Illustrator® are popular with fashion designers working in industry and specialist programs for garment design are also available. Colour working drawings of garments in a collection are compiled by certain brands or retailers into brochures from which the ranges can be sold by their sales teams (see Chapter 8).

Fashion illustrations are artistic representations of garment designs, shown on the figure. Fashion designers rarely have time to produce illustrations of their designs, which can be disappointing as fashion illustration is an outlet for their artistic talents. Illustrations of final ranges may be used to present work to clients. Fashion illustrations are used frequently by designers in the presentation of personal portfolios to emphasise the creativity of their design ideas (see Chapter 18). When fashion illustrations are used in the promotion of ranges, such as advertising or in-store posters, it is usual to commission a specialist fashion

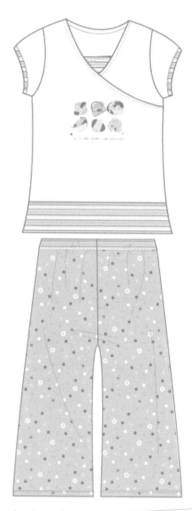

Fig. 4.2 Working drawing of girls' nightwear using Adobe® Illustrator
Courtesy of Nina Faresin

illustrator to do this, rather than the person who originally designed the product (see Chapter 3).

Pattern cutting and specification sheets

A selected amount of the designer's drawings are made up into samples, either by sample machinists within the design studio or by machinists within factories. To enable these samples to be made, patterns are produced for which either the designer or pattern cutter may be responsible (see Chapter 5). A knowledge of pattern cutting is a great source of inspiration to designers as it provides a vast range of techniques and ideas for style and design details. This forms part of the signature style of certain ready-to-wear designers, including Sophia Kokosalaki's use of draping and Hussein Chalayan's complex seaming. To communicate the information effectively to the machinist, the designer (or a production assistant in some ready-to-wear companies) usually produces a specification sheet (spec. sheet) containing an accurate working drawing and details of fabric, trims, components and stitching requirements. Brands or retailers with in-house design teams produce 'design packs' consisting of spec. sheets of garments, which are put into work with appropriate suppliers by product developers or buyers.

Range presentations

For branded labels and the mass market, visual and verbal presentations often have to be given by designers to explain and justify their designs. In the mass market, designers working for garment suppliers present a specified range of illustrations, working drawings or sample garments to the buyer with a verbal justification for their inclusion in the retailer's range. They may be accompanied by the supplier's sales executive to discuss cost prices, quantities and delivery. Dealing with buyers is similar in some aspects to presenting design work as a student to lecturers in a crit except that the buyer ultimately has the power to select the final range for the retailer. The buyer makes the decision as to whether the designer's garments will be sold and can therefore have a large financial impact on the supplier. So, while the designer must be willing to explain the reasons their ideas could be successful, they must do so diplomatically without overstepping the mark towards an argument, due to the potentially negative consequences for the company and their own jobs. Designers who have positive relationships with buyers for major companies are in demand and may be sought after by competing suppliers.

Range development meetings

After a final range of garments has been selected and initial orders have been placed, designers can work closely with colleagues in other roles within the company to enable the products to be developed to meet the necessary quality and fit standards in bulk production. At ready-to-wear or branded level designers may liaise with the garment manufacturers, either directly or through production assistants or production managers, as the development of the range progresses. In mass market garment suppliers the designer may hand over the development of the range to a pattern cutter, garment technologist or product developer at this stage. The designer of the range may meet the buyer of the product several times for range development meetings before production commences, discussing the progress of garment features such as colour, print and design details. Garment technologists and fabric technologists can also be involved in the meetings to discuss technical aspects of the styles (see Chapters 6 and 7).

Fashion shows

Many ready-to-wear designers hold twice-yearly fashion shows as the major method of promoting the range to buyers and the fashion press. In order to do this they require the services of art directors, choreographers and stylists (see Chapter 15). Designers are likely to be involved in the preparations for the shows to ensure that all garment samples are ready on time and the design team may also be busy backstage at the show, helping to dress models with the correct garments and accessories. *London Fashion Week*, organised by the British Fashion Council, takes place in January and September each year, showcasing ready-to-wear runway shows, supported by an exhibition where designer ranges are sold to retailers. Some of the major fashion retailers also organise fashion shows to present new garment ranges to their sales staff.

WHERE DO FASHION DESIGNERS WORK?

The following types of company employ fashion designers:

- designer labels (couture, ready-to-wear or diffusion);
- branded labels (products sold under the name of the brand rather than the retailer);
- manufacturers/suppliers;
- retailers (where products are sold under the store's own label).

For ready-to-wear and branded ranges' design teams there is an emphasis on trend research and drawing design ideas. In manufacturers' design teams there can be more opportunity to use technical skills. The number of fashion design positions in the middle market and mass market far outweigh the tiny proportion of jobs available at designer level, although the amount of press coverage the catwalk shows receive may give the opposite impression.

Designer labels

The term 'couture' is sometimes mistakenly used as a catch-all term to describe all 'designer' ranges, but in practice it has a strict definition. Couture designers must have an *atelier* (studio) based in Paris. Couture garments are one-offs in that they are fitted to the customer's own measurements and sewn mostly by hand. The clientele is limited to a few hundred people world-wide as prices are often in excess of £10 000 per outfit. Perhaps surprisingly, many couture houses fail to make a profit, but a couture range is crucial to the brand's promotional strategy. Personalised fittings, expensive fabrics and catwalk shows which often cost more than £100 000 all contribute to the high price of couture garments. The costs of the fashion show can be recouped by extensive press coverage, which may be worth more than spending the equivalent money on advertising. This is the conduit by which the general public, who would never dream of purchasing a couture garment, buy into this glamorous world by purchasing licensed products such as perfume and accessories, providing world-wide mass market sales which in turn fund the fashion shows.

Ready-to-wear (*prêt-à-porter*) refers to garments at 'designer' level which are mass-produced and less expensive than couture ranges, with the most publicity given to shows in Milan, Paris, London and New York. The costs of staging fashion shows, advertising and the high quality of design, pattern cutting, fabric and manufacture result in ready-to-wear garments costing more than high street products. The fact that ready-to-wear ranges are usually manufactured in smaller quantities than mass-market products also contributes towards the higher price bracket, as this can reduce cost-effectiveness in production. However, those designers who are very successful commercially can produce garments in large volumes. Some of the garments on the runway will never be produced for sale, either because no buyers select them or they are not feasible to produce in multiple quantities, but they may serve a vital purpose of gaining publicity for the label. It is an open secret that most high street retailers derive much of their inspiration from ready-to-wear collections. Though these retailers are unlikely to be able to gain access to the runway shows, the ranges can be viewed prior to being sold in shops, via the internet and magazines, allowing the mass market to develop versions of key catwalk trends often within the same season (Goworek 2001).

Many ready-to-wear designers also produce diffusion ranges aimed at a wider market than their main lines, which are usually a contraction of the designer's name such as D&G (by Dolce & Gabanna). Because they have broader appeal to consumers, and may be made from less expensive fabrics, diffusion ranges can be made in larger quantities than ready-to-wear, making them more cost-effective to produce and therefore more competitively priced. Due to the high financial rewards involved on both sides, designer collaborations with high street retailers have become routine in the UK. Pioneered by Marks & Spencer and Debenhams, garment collections by ready-to-wear designers are mass-manufactured exclusively for the retailer. As these ranges are substantially cheaper than those shown on the catwalk they do not compete directly but increase coverage of the designer's name and provide a regular income which can assist in financing the fashion show.

Branded labels

This area of the market refers to ranges which are not generally shown on the catwalk but command higher prices than most mass market fashion. Branded companies do not usually manufacture or retail their own products but sell them mainly through independent stores and department stores. Exceptions to this rule include French Connection and Diesel who sell branded goods to other stores in addition to their own retail outlets. One of the reasons that branded labels cost more than the mass market is that three companies need to make a profit out of the retail selling price, i.e. the manufacturer, brand and retailer, whereas most high street fashion stores buy directly from their suppliers. This makes the branded company a 'middleman' similar to a wholesale operation, though the

Fig. 4.3 The business structure of a branded label

organisation has a significant role to play as it is responsible for the generation of the designs, placing orders with manufacturers and promoting the brand (see Fig. 4.3). Designers for branded labels tend to have more creative freedom in their roles than those designing for mass market retailers, due to the higher price bracket, which gives them a wider choice of fabrics and trims.

Manufacturers/suppliers

The majority of fashion design jobs in the UK are with manufacturers or suppliers, as they are more likely than retailers to have design departments. Most UK-based suppliers in the fashion industry now use offshore manufacture and usually do not own the factories with which they work. Some garment and footwear manufacturers remain in the UK, notably jerseywear and tailoring factories, but this area has diminished greatly since the 1970s, in the wake of more competitively-priced imports. Many companies now manufacture the goods abroad whilst keeping the design and sales activity based in this country, typically consisting of a head of design managing designers for specific retail accounts. The supplier also requires pattern cutters, graders and sample machinists to develop the garment range and these positions may be based within the design team or overseas in the factories used by the company (see Chapter 5).

Some retailers provide the manufacturer with a package of designs. The manufacturer's design team then makes the patterns and provides sample garments to the retailer's specifications. A few retailers make their own patterns in-house and request garment samples from their suppliers. Large suppliers may have more departments than smaller companies, with specialised roles within a team (see Fig. 4.4). Smaller companies usually require particularly versatile designers to perform multiple roles, e.g. designer/pattern cutter/product developer.

To submit an accurate cost price the manufacturer requires detailed information from the designer of the product about design details, finishes, fabric quality, fastenings etc. as every component of a design has cost implications. Designers therefore need to be methodical and decisive in documenting their requirements for every element of a garment. Suppliers' sales executives negotiate finalised prices with buyers before orders are confirmed, which sometimes involves amendments to the design or materials to achieve the buyer's target price (see

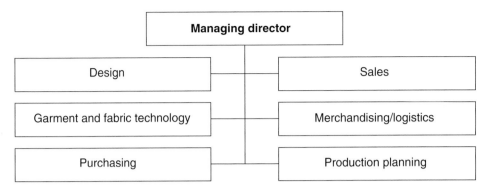

Fig. 4.4 Typical departmental structure of a UK garment supplier

Fig. 4.5 The business structure of a multiple fashion retailer

Chapter 8). The designer is likely to be involved in the process if the style needs amending in some way which could entail changing the fabric or reducing the design detail. Designers' original design concepts are frequently compromised for financial reasons, and if amendments are not made to a style to get it into price the buyer may not place an order for the product. Buyers also frequently request changes to designs if they believe these alterations will make the product more commercially appealing. The main aim of the supplier is obviously to make money and, consequently, designers' creative ideas are considered to be secondary to the company's profitability. It is therefore essential for designers to be flexible when developing garments for high street retailers.

Retailers

Most fashion retailers in the UK do not employ their own design teams, mainly because this adds substantial costs to the company's overheads, which can result in higher selling prices or lower profits. Instead they rely mainly on designers who work for their suppliers, with whom they work closely (see Fig. 4.5). Certain fashion retailers sell products designed exclusively by their own in-house design teams including Karen Millen, Oasis, George, Adams and Next. Some retailers, such as Topshop and New Look, select products from their in-house designers as well as developing ideas with their suppliers. Marks & Spencer have a design team at their head office who brief their suppliers' designers with the styling and colour trends for their ranges.

FASHION-RELATED DESIGN ROLES

Knitwear design

A knitwear designer is in effect a fashion designer responsible for developing both the fabric and styling of knitted garments. Knitwear designers select the yarns from which the knitwear is made from yarn suppliers through sales agents or trade fairs, such as *Pitti Filati* in Florence. Technical knowledge of knitted fabric construction is essential in this job. Many fashion students decide to incorporate knitwear and woven garments into their degree collections and this can enhance their employment opportunities as they may be able to apply for jobs designing either of these product types after graduation. Knitwear designers are more likely than designers of woven garments to use CAD within their jobs as the electronic knitting machines which are used for bulk production are compatible with CAD programs. The knitwear industry is more advanced than other parts of the clothing industry in its technological developments. 'Whole garment' machines have recently been developed in Japan to produce complete knitted garments which require no sewing (see Fig. 4.6). This technology is being used by UK-based manufacturers to avoid relatively high labour costs and is more economical in the use of yarn as there is no wastage. Garment production can therefore be located closer to the retailers with a quicker turnaround time.

Fig. 4.6 WholeGarment Shima Seiki knitting machine
Courtesy of Quantum Knitwear

Corporatewear design

Designers are also needed to create ideas for corporate wear and workwear for organisations including airlines, banks, retailers, the armed forces and the catering trade. This is not strictly fashion design as the styles are classic and functional, but it is an area in which the skills of a fashion designer can be used, especially those with strong technical abilities. Some high profile businesses have employed ready-to-wear designers to create corporate clothing which has gained them publicity in the press, such as Julien Macdonald's designs for British Airways cabin staff in 2000. From a production viewpoint corporatewear is much more cost-effective to manufacture than frequently changing styles of fashion garments as they are usually made in large quantities in the same style over a relatively long period of time. Various manufacturers and retailers are dedicated to corporatewear, either being commissioned to produce staff uniforms by companies or retailing their own designs.

Costume design

Costume designers can design for TV, stage or film for futuristic, contemporary or period productions. Costume designers can come from a fashion or textiles background and graduates in embroidery are sought after in this field as their skills are particularly applicable to the design of ornate period costumes. The roles of costume designers and fashion designers both require design and technical skills, though for costume designers there is usually more emphasis on knowledge of historical clothing. Costume design can be a highly creative role as it is not necessary to work within the same commercial constraints as fashion designers since the garments are not intended for sale to the general public, though they must appeal to the audience. However, costume designers still need to work within a specific budget and timescale. Costume designers can hire or buy costumes or have them made to their own specifications if sufficient budget is available. TV presenters' outfits may also be selected by costume designers. Theatres, TV and film production companies usually keep their own stockrooms of costumes, which costume designers or wardrobe staff are responsible for maintaining, and which may hire out clothing to other companies. Many costume designers work on a freelance basis (see Chapter 17), being hired by production companies to work on specific plays, programmes or films.

CAREER ROUTES

Graduates should expect to work as assistant fashion designers initially, being allocated tasks by an experienced designer. Some companies also employ design room assistants who help the design team in basic tasks and they will not necessarily progress to become designers themselves. A fashion degree is not essential for this role and the salary is usually the lowest one in the design department, but graduates may consider applying for this type of position to learn how a design room operates with a view to applying for assistant designer vacancies. An assistant designer may be given responsibility for designing part of a range as well as helping the designer with tasks from preparing storyboards to pressing sample garments ready for presentations. Many adverts for fashion designers request applicants with three years experience or more. Several international ready-to-wear labels are subsidiaries of larger companies such as LVMH and Gucci Group, who provide recruitment details online.

The next level in a designer's career could be as a design manager, or head of design in some companies. The salary for a manager is often substantially better than that of a designer because of the additional management tasks involved, but some people may prefer to remain as designers throughout their careers as there is likely to be less design involved in a manager's position. The highest level within a design department is often a director's position. In the mass market this offers the maximum salary but may involve little or no hands-on design. In a ready-to-wear company however, the design director usually continues to design as well as managing and directing the design team, specifying the looks for each season's collection. Fashion designers' salaries can be within a wide range. Within retailers, they can be equivalent to buyers and merchandisers' salaries, but some designers may be paid more highly if employed by suppliers.

Though many educational institutions in the UK offer fashion degrees, the most famous are Central Saint Martins (CSM) and the Royal College of Art (RCA), both based in London. CSM offers undergraduate and postgraduate courses in fashion and textiles-related subjects. The RCA offers only postgraduate courses. Some of the world's top designers have studied at these institutions, some having progressed from CSM to the RCA. Alumni (graduates from a certain institution) who have gone on to design ready-to-wear collections include Stella McCartney, Sophia Kokosalaki, Phoebe Philo (formerly Chief Designer at Chloe in Paris) and Alexander McQueen from CSM; and Julien Mcdonald, Brian Kirby (of Boudicca) and Christopher Bailey (design director of Burberry) from the RCA.

It is generally acknowledged that UK fashion design students are highly innovative and consequently this can make graduates sought after internationally. It is also possible, though fairly rare, for ready-to-wear designers to graduate from courses outside London. Many other countries have their own key fashion courses, notably including the Parsons School of Design in New York, where alumni include Marc Jacobs and Narciso Rodriguez as well as British designer Jasper Conran. The Fashion Institute of Technology (FIT) in New York is also well-known and Michael Kors (who designs the Celine range as well as his own collection) studied there. Other courses renowned for producing catwalk designers include Bunka Fashion College in Tokyo, whose alumni include Yohji Yamamoto and Junya Watanabe, and the Royal Academy of Fine Arts in Antwerp, where Ann Demeulemeester and Dries van Noten studied fashion design.

Despite the many famous names mentioned here, it is a statistical fact that the majority of fashion graduates on these courses, and on the hundreds of other fashion courses, will not become well-known. However, they will have opportunities to apply for design jobs in areas other than designer level or in a wide variety of creatively-orientated roles within the fashion industry.

In the UK, current government policy which aims to place half of all young people in higher education by 2010, has resulted in increasing quantities of students graduating each year and competing for a relatively static number of jobs in the fashion and textiles industry. Fashion design is the most widespread degree within fashion and textiles, being offered by 33 educational institutions across the UK (ucas.ac.uk, 2005). Entry requirements, aspects of the course content and reputation can vary, so potential students should investigate a selection of courses before deciding where to apply. It is widely acknowledged in industry that the volume of fashion design graduates greatly exceeds the number of jobs available for designers. A high proportion of fashion designers work in womenswear, but this is an intensively competitive area in which to find a job and there is often greater demand for menswear, childrenswear, knitwear, lingerie and accessories designers. There are specialist courses such as BA (Hons) Product Design and Development at the London College of Fashion where students can focus on either footwear or accessories. There is one specialist knitwear degree in the UK, at Nottingham Trent University, though various fashion design and textile design courses include knitwear within the curriculum. There are currently four degree courses in costume design in the UK, the most well-known being at Wimbledon School of Art.

CASE STUDIES

Ready-to-wear designer

Career path

Mark Eley and Wakako Kishimoto established their own ready-to-wear collection in 1995 and the husband-and-wife team have been described in the press as 'one of the success stories of British fashion'. Their range, renowned for its use of vivid and original abstract prints, has been shown on the runway at London Fashion Week since 2001. Their fluid integration of garment styling and print was inspired by studying degree courses which combined clothing and fabric design: Mark studied Fashion and Weave and Wakako studied Fashion and Print. The duo first met on work placement in New York and have been designing prints together since 1992. They have collaborated with an extensive selection of international designers including Jil Sander, Marc Jacobs, Louis Vuitton, Yves St Laurent, Nicole Farhi and Alexander McQueen. In 2002 they were commissioned to design a clothing range for New Look, who sponsored their catwalk show that year. They have also recently produced a collection for sportswear company Ellesse. Eley Kishimoto's print design expertise has been applied to products as diverse as tables, chairs, luggage, wallpaper, ceramics, glass, lingerie, footwear and sunglasses. The significance of their work was demonstrated by a retrospective show at the Victoria and Albert Museum (V&A) in 2003, looking back at the first ten years of their collaborative work. The V&A described 'their effortless combination of interior design and fashion' as being 'reminiscent of the holistic approach adopted by designers during the Art Deco period'.

Role and responsibilities

Mark is managing director of the business (see Fig. 4.7) and Wakako is the creative director. Mark says they need to be 'chameleons' to take on various roles when needed, from the more glamorous aspects such as organising fashion shows and talking to the press, through to everyday tasks like collecting the team's lunch and packing boxes to get orders out on time. He explains:

> *Our designs are inspired by everyday life and our notions of what we feel is current. We want to tell a story through our collections. We find inspiration as quickly as possible because designing is only a minor element within our calendar.*

Seeing those designs through to reality usually takes about eight months, most of which is spent developing the range for production. This means working on more than one season's collection at a time. Mark and Wakako's roles include sourcing fabrics, working on sample garments and co-ordinating the ranges as well as filling in for other jobs when required. They have built up relationships with many of the 210 stores which stock their ready-to-wear range. Mark spent three days a week for three months working in the Eley Kishimoto shop in Bermondsey when it first opened, so he has first-hand knowledge of the customers who wear the range.

Mark works closely with the team, which can vary from 25 to 30 people at the busiest periods. The company's Brixton premises incorporate a design room, cutting room and print room. Sample lengths of their signature designs are printed there to use in the garments shown on the runway. The fabrics which go into production to be sold in stores are then produced by outside sources. Specialist pattern-cutters are employed to perfect the fit of the garments which Mark describes as 'a luxury we have invested in because mistakes can cause financial

Fig. 4.7 Mark Eley judging students' work at the Texprint exhibition 2005 Courtesy of Texprint. Photo by James McCauley

headaches'. Like many other UK designer ranges, some Eley Kishimoto garments are manufactured in Italy, due to the high quality of make-up and their ability to produce relatively small bulk quantities.

Career advice

Mark is closely involved with fashion design education as he has been a visiting lecturer and is currently an external assessor. Eley Kishimoto employ fashion and textiles graduates who have usually been personally recommended to them or have worked there on placement. The main qualities Mark says he looks for when taking on a graduate are 'personality, work motivation and a sense of humour'. He advises students to 'consider an alternative plan' after graduation, rather than expecting to immediately launch a ready-to-wear label. He adds:

> Students should be aware of their abilities and what they can achieve to allow them to realise their potential.

Knitwear designer for a garment manufacturer

Career path

Lucy Childs has been a designer at Quantum Knitwear, a womenswear manufacturer based in Hinckley, for four years (see Fig. 4.8). She studied a BSc (Hons) Textile Design sandwich course where she specialised in knitwear, graduating in 2001 with a first class honours degree. Her work placement year was spent at Courtaulds Knitwear (later bought by the Sara Lee Corporation). Six months after graduation Lucy joined Davenport Knitwear, which was sold in 2004 to its current owner, the Quantum Clothing Group.

Fig. 4.8 Lucy Childs in the Quantum Knitwear design studio

Role and responsibilities

Lucy lists her main responsibilities as:

- identifying future trends;
- yarn and trim sourcing;
- compiling comparative shop reports in the UK and abroad;
- designing new stitch and swatch ideas as inspiration for garment ideas;
- meeting customers;
- arranging for sample garments to be made;
- designing new ideas;
- organising lab dips for yarn;
- fitting garments.

Quantum Knitwear manufactures garments in the UK using whole garment machinery, so it is no longer necessary for them to employ machinists to stitch the garments together. The company used standard electronic knitting machines until recently and the designers have developed the skills to design products suitable for this new technology. Lucy sources and develops yarns by meeting spinners and yarn agents. She designs for two of the company's accounts, Oasis and Next, and her fellow designer, Colleen Walsh, designs for Laura Ashley and Marks & Spencer (see Fig. 4.9). The technical designer, Michelle Wylly, has a role similar to that of a garment technologist (see Chapter 7), working closely with Lucy and Colleen on styles which have been ordered by retailers, co-ordinating the production and approval of garments at various stages, including sampling, grading and production. Quantum Knitwear's Head of Design, Lynn Bale, is responsible for ensuring that her team design garments which are profitable for the company, as well as designing products herself.

For design ideas to be made into garments, Lucy explains that she requests samples to be issued by the knitting machine programmers within the factory:

> *All details need to be included at this stage – measurements, yarn type, sketches, etc. Excellent communication is needed between design and the programmers to ensure that the sample is knitted correctly – in whole garment knitting this can be a lengthy process!*

For design meetings with buyers, Lucy usually takes image boards with tear sheets, samples of knitted fabric or garments, and hand-drawn sketches of new

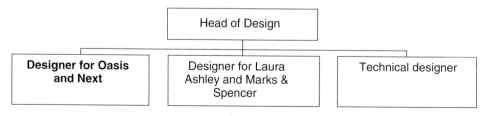

Fig. 4.9 Structure of the design team at Quantum Knitwear

garment designs. Being based in the same country as their customers means that Quantum has relatively short lead times for a knitwear supplier, enabling them to design garments which can potentially be sampled within two days and delivered to the retailer within two months. Lucy organises lab dips by sending colours to the dyers or yarn spinners for garments which will go into bulk production (see Chapter 6). She also participates in garment fittings:

> *I'm very involved in the fitting process for Oasis. As Oasis are a design-led business they need me involved to help technically from the start.*

Lucy is in regular contact with buyers at Next and Oasis. She has many other tasks relating to aspects of garment production and works closely with other colleagues in the factory including the technical director, production director, production manager, sales director and merchandisers. She travels to *Pitti Filati* twice a year, to pick up new trends, networking and building relationships with current suppliers and customers and developing new contacts. She also visits New York, Paris, Barcelona and Milan to find inspiration for her designs or to see spinners. Lucy describes her favourite aspects of the job as well as the challenges she faces:

> *I like travelling, doing shop reports and meeting customers. I enjoy sketching and designing new ideas and the satisfaction of seeing my design go from a sketch into production and into store. It's very rewarding if I see someone in a jumper I've designed or if it appears in a magazine. I also enjoy seeing the garments in various stages throughout the factory – an advantage of our production being UK-based. It's difficult to remember everything as there seems to be so much going on in the factory in which we are all involved! It can also be hard to convey ideas and information to the programmers as we need to be so clear and go through things step by step.*

Lucy says that teamwork is 'vital throughout the factory all of the time' and she adds 'everyone in the team is so busy you have to be able to motivate yourself'. She finds communication skills essential for dealing with customers and suppliers, helped by the use of email. She also uses Microsoft Word and Excel for creating size specifications and compiling other information. She rates planning and organisational skills as 'very important' and writes lists of tasks to enable her to meet deadlines. Her major organisational responsibility is to liaise with the knitting machine programmers, dyers and finishers to ensure that samples are received on time for her customers. Lucy also says:

> *Creativity and technical skills are very important as you must constantly come up with new ideas and you need a good background in knitting and garment construction to be a knitwear designer.*

Career advice

Lucy recommends finding work experience to help students to establish their careers:

My placement year was so beneficial and an excellent starting block for future jobs. It was a great introduction to working in a factory environment. They were also manufacturing in the Far East so I gained experience in sending sketches and specs there.

Recruiting designers for Quantum Knitwear is the responsibility of Lucy's line manager, Lynn, who says she looks for creative, hard-working team players with a friendly, confident personality. Lucy advises prospective designers:

You need to be very dedicated and motivated to have a career in this industry as it can be difficult and stressful at times. The hours can be long and unpredictable so you have to be very committed. You need to be confident in your own abilities as it can be very challenging and competitive especially when trying to sell an idea to a customer. Don't be disheartened by the number of jobs available in the industry. Be persistent – I got my job after sending my CV in for a higher position. When a lower position became available I called the sales director and eventually got the job.

FURTHER READING

Books

Goworek, H. (2001) *Fashion Buying.* Blackwell Publishing, Oxford.
Jenkyn Jones, S. (2002) *Fashion Design.* Laurence King, London.
Jones, T. and Mair, A. (2001) *Fashion Now.* Taschen, Cologne.
McKelvey, K. and Munslow, J. (2003) *Fashion Design: Process, Innovation and Practice.* Blackwell Publishing, Oxford.
McRobbie, A. (1998) *British Fashion Design: Rag Trade or Image Industry?* Routledge, London.

Magazines and newspapers

Coulson, C. (2004) Charming Prints. *The Daily Telegraph,* 14 September, London (telegraph.co.uk)
Jackson, L. (2004) Eley Kishimoto. *Icon Magazine,* Issue 15, September, London (iconmagazine.co.uk)

Websites

www.dti.gov.uk/support/textiles/designers.htm to download a copy of 'A Study of the UK Designer Fashion Sector: Findings and Recommendations'.
www.londonfashionweek.co.uk
www.ucas.ac.uk

Pattern cutting 5

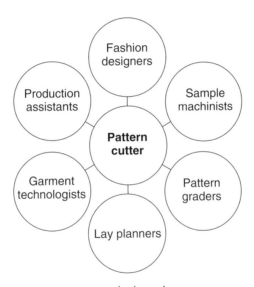

Fig. 5.1 Liaison between pattern cutters and other roles

Pattern cutting is a craft which transforms the fashion designer's ideas from two-dimensional concepts into three-dimensional reality. Pattern cutting can be combined with the fashion designer's role, as a vital component of the product development process or it can be a job in its own right. It may also be part of the role of a garment technologist within a clothing manufacturer. Most pattern cutters are employed by garment suppliers, based either within a UK office alongside design and sales or within factories overseas. Ready-to-wear labels are invariably responsible for making their own patterns to maintain control of the whole design process. Patterns for ready-to-wear garments are cut either by the design team, in-house pattern cutters (see case study in this chapter) or freelancers.

Because pattern cutters are not necessarily required all year round at designer level due to the seasonal nature and size of the business, a full-time pattern cutting position may not be required, so freelancers who probably work for several designer labels can be employed at appropriate times. Highly skilled freelance pattern cutters are sought after and well-paid, as the cut of the garments is crucial in a designer range where the customer expects excellent quality and fit to justify the price tag. As stated in Chapter 4, a limited number of fashion retailers have their own design teams, including pattern cutters, enabling them to develop garments quickly in-house.

Patterns are usually developed from working drawings supplied by designers. Designers who cut their own patterns do not need detailed working drawings for this purpose as they know the look they are hoping to achieve and are able to design within the pattern cutting process. A designer employed by a garment supplier may work alongside the pattern cutter, enabling them to discuss any questions about patterns. It is an increasingly frequent scenario to have a designer working for a retailer or supplier in the UK, handing over a working drawing through an intermediary such as a sales executive or production assistant to a pattern cutter who is based at a clothing factory in another country. It is therefore vital that the working drawing is crystal-clear, supported by notes to clarify design details. This visual and written communication between designers and pattern cutters is essential in order to minimise the number of garment samples required before the fit of a garment is improved, thereby increasing the company's profitability.

FLAT PATTERN-CUTTING

Flat pattern cutting is the customary method used in the fashion industry. First, patterns are developed in the retailer or brand's standard size, which is usually a UK 12 (European 38/40 or US 8/10) for womenswear. As a starting point, basic blocks can be constructed by following standard measurement instructions, from which patterns for any feasible garment style can be developed (see Fig. 5.2).

Basic blocks are adapted in a first draft to reflect the required fit and relevant details for a garment design by tracing onto transparent paper or by using a tracing wheel on card. Students are sometimes taught to cut patterns using fifth-scale blocks for speed and economy, but in practice in industry full-scale blocks are always used. The edges of the blocks on the first draft are where the seams of the garment will meet, so a working pattern is traced off with seam allowances varying from 0.5 cm to 1.5 cm added around the edges to enable the product to be sewn together.

The size of the seam allowances depends on the type of machinery and fabric to be used, indicated by adding small notches near the corners of the pattern. Pattern cutters need to be very neat and thorough with attention to detail. They work with precise measurements and if they do not use the correct seam allowance, the fit and quality of the production garments can be adversely

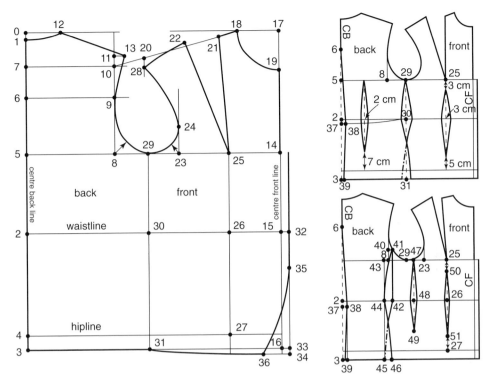

Fig. 5.2 The tailored jacket block
Courtesy of Winifred Aldrich

affected, resulting in high returns and poor sales. Pattern cutters need a thorough understanding of the construction of garments. Pattern cutting author Winifred Aldrich considers awareness of fabric and the target market to be essential qualities for pattern cutters:

My main message about following a career in pattern cutting is that a knowledge of fabric and its relationship to the pattern is fundamental. You have to have an intuitive sense when you get hold of a piece of fabric and know how it's going to fall. You should have a feeling of what sort of market you're interested in – whether you want to be involved in developing garments that thousands of people wear or for a limited number. You need to be multi-skilled to take any kind of job in the fashion trade and you have to be flexible about where you work and how you work

Various aspects of the block can be adapted to reflect the required style, including manipulating darts to affect the fit and styling (see Fig. 5.3), adding seams as design details, adding collars or revers to tops, adding fullness to skirts with gores, godets or pleats and reducing or lengthening hems. When the styling and design details on the pattern are finished, pattern pieces for facings and interfacings, which help with the finish and construction of the garment, can be added if necessary.

Fig. 5.3 Options for dart manipulation in the bodice

Patterns require the following annotation:

- reference number or name of a garment style;
- garment size;
- centre-front (CF) or centre-back line (CB);
- grainline;
- folds;
- balance marks (notches to ensure back and front pieces are sewn together correctly);
- number of pieces (to ensure none are missing);
- the name of the piece, as some parts can look very similar;
- construction lines, e.g. darts, buttonholes and pocket positions.

The 'grain' of the fabric lies parallel to the selvedge (the finished edges of the cloth where it was attached to the loom). On the pattern the grainline indicates the direction of the grain, to explain how the pattern piece should be laid on the fabric. Designers may intentionally require parts of a garment, such as a waist-band, to be placed 'on the bias', i.e. diagonally on the fabric to take advantage of the stretch properties this offers. It is important to organise the patterns well as one of the marks of a good pattern cutter is that a colleague can easily find patterns they require if the pattern cutter is out of the office.

Knitwear pattern cutting tends to be based on relatively simple shapes as there is a lot of flexibility in the fabric's stretch properties. 'Cut-and-sew' knitwear is made from pieces of knitted fabric called 'blanks' which are cut to shape then sewn together with overlockers. The garments are then finished at the neck, cuffs and hem, often using knitted ribs. Fully-fashioning is a traditional and high quality method of making knitwear with all of the pieces knitted to the finished shape, so no fabric cutting is required and there is minimal wastage.

GARMENT SAMPLES AND AMENDMENTS

When the first pattern is completed the fabric is cut out by the design room assistant, pattern cutter or designer for an initial sample to be made. Students often make 'toiles' in a substitute fabric such as calico or muslin. However, in industry even initial garment samples are usually made in the same quality of fabric that will be used in production, or the closest type available, to ensure that they accurately resemble the garments which will be sold. First samples of a wide range of garments can be made, of which a certain number will be selected to be manufactured in bulk production. After the first sample has been fitted, amendments can be made to the pattern of a style, e.g. correcting the balance of a hemline to make it hang evenly at the front and back.

Fittings usually take place at the retailer's head office at mass market level or in the design studio. Designers, pattern cutters, garment technologists and buyers can attend fittings, taking notes and discussing the fit and aesthetic aspects of the sample. A disadvantage of sourcing overseas is that pattern cutters cannot be present at regular fitting sessions, though when a buyer or garment technologist from a retailer visits the manufacturer fittings may sometimes be conducted there. Most patterns need to be amended and one or more new samples submitted before the fit of a garment is approved. Final patterns which have been made manually from card are hole-punched and hung together on a hook on a clothes rack in the design room. Production patterns which will be used to cut the bulk fabric will be based on these final patterns, so it is vital that the measurements and annotation are precise.

PATTERN CUTTING EQUIPMENT

The most basic equipment required by pattern cutters is listed below, though pattern cutters may have their own preferences about what they prefer to use. A flat, clean working surface large enough to accommodate full-size patterns is needed to work on.

- Grader square or Patternmaster.
- Ruler.
- Metre rule.
- 2H/3H pencils.
- Eraser.
- Sellotape.
- Tape measure.
- Pins.

Fig. 5.4 Accumark Silhouette software
Courtesy of Gerber Technology

- Paper scissors.
- Pattern notchers.

CAD/CAM

Computers have had much more impact on design and pattern cutting than on the manufacturing process, speeding up the cycle in which products are developed. Draping fabrics onto 3D images at the design stage can cut out the sample make-up process to show how a finished product will look, saving time and money on sampling and pattern cutting. It is now possible for retailers to select garments from computer-generated images so that a whole range of samples does not need to be produced and patterns can be developed just for styles which have been selected for production. Patterns can be drafted on a computer by digitising key points of blocks which have been produced manually, allowing easy storage of the patterns in computer files which can be printed out when required (see Fig. 5.4). Blocks can be saved and opened on the computer to produce adaptations of existing patterns. The patterns can be printed out with a plotter, a large printer which uses a pen to draw the lines of the pattern onto paper.

DRAPING

This highly creative pattern cutting technique is also known as modelling on the stand and tends to be used at couture and ready-to-wear level because of the dramatic shapes it makes and the large amounts of fabric it often uses. This three-dimensional method allows the designer to develop the pattern and design simultaneously. It is the reverse of flat pattern-cutting in that the prototype is made before the flat pattern pieces. It is suitable for styles which involve wrapping, tying, draping and gathering with fluid fabric. It is possible to develop a garment with a combination of flat pattern cutting and draping, e.g. where part of a garment such as a neckline requires a draped effect. The fabric is pinned directly onto the dressmaker's mannequin. It may also be necessary to draw lines and write on this initial sample for reference. The pattern needs to be precisely annotated, ideally with photographs to show how it should be reassembled as it may be difficult to visualise the final effect once the pattern piece is laid out.

CREATIVE PATTERN CUTTING

It is undoubtedly necessary for all pattern cutters to possess creative skills to interpret the sketches and specifications given to them by designers. The term 'creative pattern cutter' is often used when positions with garment suppliers are advertised. Sometimes this means that the pattern cutter does not work with a designer in the company, but may be asked by a retailer to make patterns based on specific samples or tear sheets. It has become standard practice for many mass market retailers to buy garments on directional shopping trips, usually from designer ranges, in order to develop a cheaper adaptation of the style. It can therefore be useful for a pattern cutter working in the mass market to acquire the skill to take a pattern from an existing garment. It is easier to do this if the bought sample can be deconstructed, but this may not be permitted and the pattern cutter may have to use the intact garment to take measurements to assist in producing the pattern.

GRADING

Design teams may have specialist graders or can combine grading with the pattern cutting role, so that the same person is responsible for seeing the process through to production. This can be essential in a small company where only one full-time person may be employed in this area, and it can also give the job more variety. A small or extremely cost-conscious supplier may expect designers also to be responsible for pattern cutting and grading within the company, although it may be difficult to find someone who is equally skilled in each of these areas. Initial samples are developed in a size which is in the middle of the full size range, so that the patterns can be graded up or down to all of the sizes required. When grading, a 'nest' of patterns is created, with lines radiating from the smaller patterns to the surrounding larger sizes. The differences between the sizes are called increments and they vary depending on the part of the garment, the type of garment and the 'grade rules' of the retailer or brand. There is usually an increment of 5 cm in total circumference between each size in the chest, waist and hip measurements. Recently several major UK retailers and universities contributed towards an extensive and costly national survey using computer body scanning equipment, but the results are confidential to the retailers involved, enabling them to update their sizing systems (Aldrich, 2004).

CAD/CAM systems tend to be used more frequently for the grading of production styles than for the development of sample patterns. A file of graded patterns can be utilised within compatible software to develop a lay plan for the most economical use of the fabric with the least possible wastage. In preparation for garment production, the bulk fabric is spread in multiple layers on a cutting table and the lay plan indicates the way in which it will be cut. A full-size printout of the lay plan is laid on top of the fabric which is cut to this template with an electric knife, resulting in bundles of individual garment pieces in varying sizes.

CAREER ROUTES

Experienced pattern cutters with strong technical skills are in demand throughout the fashion business and there is less competition in this field than within design. Pattern cutters usually start their careers at assistant or junior level, assisting experienced pattern cutters before being promoted, possibly after three or more years. They can eventually work at senior or management level and freelancing can be a lucrative option for highly skilled and experienced pattern cutters (see Chapter 17). Fashion designers sometimes move into a pattern cutting career after expanding their knowledge of patterns and garment construction in the industry. Pattern cutters can sometimes develop their careers further by moving into garment technologists' roles (see Chapter 7), giving them the option to work for fashion retailers. Pattern cutting is always included within the curriculum for fashion design courses and can also be taught separately at evening classes or summer schools at FE colleges or universities. London College of Fashion and the Kent Institute of Art and Design both offer two-year foundation degrees in pattern cutting.

CASE STUDY

Design development manager for a ready-to-wear label

Career path

Heather Fairhurst is currently design development manager for designer Paul Smith. Heather graduated from her BA (Hons) Fashion Design degree in 1987, where she produced a menswear collection in her final year. She then worked as a menswear and boyswear designer for the former Coats Viyella group until joining Paul Smith in her initial role as a technical design assistant. At this point, Heather considered carefully whether or not to move into a technical role. She admits 'I made a conscious decision not to design any more and I've never regretted it for a moment'.

Role and responsibilities

Heather manages the design development team which consists of the pattern cutters and graders for Paul Smith's menswear and womenswear ranges (see Fig. 5.5). She describes her main responsibilities as:

- meeting deadlines for pattern cutting development and grading;
- ensuring that the patterns and garments are technically viable;
- attending fitting sessions for every garment style;
- ensuring that the patterns achieve the fit that the designers are looking for;
- maintaining quality standards for the fit of Paul Smith garments;
- ensuring everyone in the team does their job successfully;
- liaising with the manufacturers who produce the garments;
- recruiting and training pattern cutters;
- managing and motivating a large, diverse team of people.

Heather is based at the company's headquarters in Nottingham and she works with various departments located there or at Paul Smith's London office, including the directors and managing director, design, production, sales and

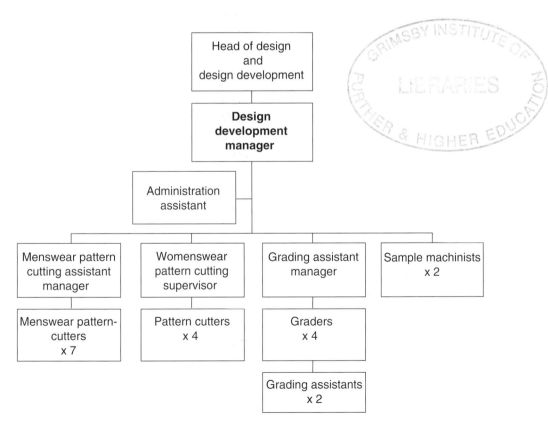

Fig. 5.5 Structure of the pattern cutting team at Paul Smith

administration. Technical design assistants liaise with the factories, supplying working drawings and specifications from which to make samples, as well as acting as technical advisers to the designers and attending pre-production fittings. The patterns are developed manually by the in-house team and when the fit is approved for a garment the patterns are passed on to the graders who grade them using a CAD/CAM system. The pattern cutters then move onto developing patterns for the next season.

Heather has travelled to clothing factories in Italy, Portugal, Morocco and India, as the garments are manufactured predominantly overseas. She attends the menswear fashion show in Paris twice a year. She has also visited Tokyo in April and October for meetings with the company which has the licence to sell the Paul Smith brand in Japan. The wide variety of responsibilities and frequent trips give Heather an extremely busy schedule so organisational skills are important to her and she remains enthusiastic about her job:

> I enjoy being involved in the development of new collections, travelling, managing the department and motivating people. I really love being in contact with the product, doing fittings and seeing new prototypes. I get a real kick out of seeing patterns being developed. Paul Smith is a very open company: you're encouraged to be yourself, which improves your flow of creativity and helps you to get a lot out of people.

The company offers training courses for managers and Heather finds dealing with personnel issues can be the most difficult part of her management role. She says teamwork is 'absolutely crucial', e.g. two pattern cutters working on products for a particular collection, such as the main Paul Smith line or the PS diffusion line would need to spread the work evenly between themselves. Heather describes her team as 'close-knit and co-operative' which she considers to be the biggest strength of any department within a company. Technical skills are obviously essential for the pattern cutters as well as creative skills. All the design patterns are cut by hand and computers are only used within the department for everyday communication including email and spreadsheets. Heather describes planning and organisational skills as essential in her role as she has to plan for seven different garment lines simultaneously.

Career advice

When recruiting graduates Heather says she looks for applicants 'who are willing to learn and whose final collections demonstrate a natural aptitude for pattern cutting'. She sets interviewees a pattern cutting test for evidence of their technical abilities and looks for people who genuinely want to be pattern cutters, rather than just using it as a route in to a designer company. However, the company does not often take on new graduates, partly because she says 'there don't seem to be many who want to go straight into pattern cutting'. Heather usually employs experienced pattern cutters, as she believes it can take six years just to learn what she calls 'the bare bones' of the craft. She thinks there is an advantage in recruiting students straight after graduation who can be trained into the company's way of working. Heather offers the following advice for students considering a career as a pattern cutter:

If you really want to do it, stick at it. Get the most out of the course you're on and use it to your advantage. Take pattern cutting seriously even if you want to become a designer, as an understanding of it will improve your design skills tenfold. Pattern cutting is 50 per cent of the design process. There is an international shortage of really good technical people.

FURTHER READING

Books

Aldrich, W. (2006), *Metric Pattern Cutting for Menswear*. Fourth edition. Blackwell Publishing, Oxford.

Aldrich, W. (2004), *Metric Pattern Cutting*. Fourth edition. Blackwell Publishing, Oxford.

Aldrich, W. (1999), *Metric Pattern Cutting for Childrenswear and Babywear*. Third edition. Blackwell Publishing, Oxford.

Aldrich, W. (1996) *Fabric, Form and Flat Pattern Cutting*. Blackwell Publishing, Oxford.

Beazley, A. and Bond, T. (2003) *Computer-Aided Pattern Design and Product Development*. Blackwell Publishing, Oxford.

Haggar, A. (2004) *Pattern Cutting for Lingerie, Beachwear and Leisurewear*. Second edition. Blackwell Publishing, Oxford.

Websites

www.gerbertechnology.com
www.lectra.com
www.morplan.com

Fabric technology 6

Fig. 6.1 Liaison between fabric technologists and other roles

Fabric technologists are responsible for ensuring that the fabrics and other components from which fashion and textiles products are made can achieve the quality standards required by fashion retailers. Fabric technologists are mostly employed by garment or fabric suppliers and they can also work for independent testing laboratories. A few large fashion retailers, such as Marks & Spencer and Next employ their own fabric technologists to liaise with their counterparts in the supply chain. In most other retail multiples, garment technologists are responsible for approving the technical aspects of fabrics. Fabric technologists are often involved in sourcing and developing fabrics with designers and buyers, and are responsible for checking the quality of fabrics and components at the initial sampling stage and in bulk production. They may specialise in knitted or woven fabrics or a combination of these, often depending on the size and product area of the company they work for. Fabric technologists may focus on menswear, womenswear or childrenswear or specific product types.

FABRIC TESTING

After a product range has been selected by a retailer's buying team, elements of each style have to be developed and finalised in preparation for bulk production. The fabric for garments is usually made to order and fabric technologists are involved in checking that the fabric manufacturer adheres to all of the relevant quality procedures. Initial garments selected by the retailer are usually made in sample fabric with substitute colours or prints. Fashion retailers' testing requirements and standards vary, but most request a sample for testing purposes of the correct fabric quality from which the selected garments will be manufactured. As retailers rarely have in-house testing facilities, most fabric testing for the high street is carried out by specialist inspection and testing labs in the UK or the country where the garments are produced, accredited by the retailer's fabric technology or quality control (QC) department. Garment manufacturers are usually expected to pay for fabric testing. Occasionally, large garment suppliers have their own in-house labs approved to the retailers' standards as this can be more economical than the expense of sending out every fabric to an independent lab. Textile testing labs are audited regularly to ensure that they adhere to the required standards and procedures. Labs such as Intertek-Labtest (see Fig. 6.2) employ fabric technologists and textile testing technicians to carry out rigorous physical tests on fabric to simulate within a short period the long-term wear and tear which will be faced by the finished garment which can include:

- abrasion;
- pilling;

Fig. 6.2 Tear-strength testing by an independent laboratory's textile technician
Courtesy of Intertek-Labtest

- colour fastness to wet and dry rubbing, washing, perspiration and light;
- tear strength;
- tensile strength.

Fabric technologists from suppliers and retailers can compare the fabric test results to the required standards. If the sample does not meet these standards the fabric technologist can discuss with the fabric supplier how the fabric can be improved or in extreme cases whether a different type of fabric should be used instead. If neither of these options is viable, the fabric technologist may recommend that the garment manufacturer should seek a different fabric source. After fabric testing, the retailer issues washing instructions to be printed in the garment label. Some retailers also require bulk fabrics to be tested to ensure that they are of the same standard as the sample fabric, and garment suppliers' fabric technologists are responsible for arranging these tests. Any issues which need to be addressed about the quality of the fabric are then discussed with the retailer's technologist.

APPROVAL OF LAB DYES AND STRIKE-OFFS

Buyers of own-label ranges normally ask for prints to be coloured or fabrics to be dyed to shades from the retailer's colour palette. The fabric manufacturer is requested to dye a swatch of the selected fabric to match the retailer's shade, known as a 'lab dye' (or 'lab dip'), which is then sent to the buyer for approval. Prints which are recoloured and printed in a sample length are called 'strike-offs'. Fabric technologists are responsible for checking that no banned dyestuffs are used, in accordance with recent European legislation. The buyer and retail fabric technologist may both look at lab dyes and strike-offs in a light box (a small booth containing light bulbs of the type used in the retailer's stores). They should be compared to the original colour swatches and may also be viewed alongside approved lab dyes of other fabrics dyed to the same shade, to see how the fabrics will look next to each other in store. If a lab dye or strike-off is rejected, the buyer and fabric technologist can give specific feedback to the fabric manufacturer about the reasons for this decision so that a further submission can be made. It is important that retailers approve colours centrally because garments merchandised together in stores are usually made in a variety of fabric types and may have been manufactured in different countries. The buyer or fabric technologist notes whether the lab dye or strike-off is approved or rejected and keeps it for reference. If approved, the fabric supplier can proceed to dye or print the bulk cloth.

FABRIC SOURCING

Fabric sourcing involves the selection of fabrics for sampling and bulk production of fashion merchandise. Designers and fabric technologists working for garment

Table 6.1 Major fabric trade fairs

Trade fair	Location and timing	Exhibitors
Première Vision	Paris – February and September	Mainly European fabric manufacturers
Indigo	Paris – February and September	Print designers
TexWorld	Paris – March and September	Fabric manufacturers from 40 countries throughout the world
Interstoff Asia	Hong Kong – October	Asian fabric manufacturers
Interfilière	Paris – February, Lyon – September	European lingerie fabric and componentry suppliers

suppliers or fashion retailers often collaborate when sourcing fabrics and this can also be part of a fashion buyer's role. Fabrics can be sourced through any of the following routes:

- trade fairs (see Table 6.1);
- visiting fabric manufacturers' offices;
- meetings with sales representatives or agents (see Chapter 8);
- fabric manufacturers' websites;
- visiting fabric mills;
- fabric merchants.

To gain knowledge of fabric manufacturers and their products, fabric technologists visit fabric fairs (often accompanied by colleagues from design or buying) and invite sales representatives and agents to meetings to show fabric ranges.

Printed fabrics

As well as establishing the construction of the fabric which is to be used for a garment style, its surface colour and pattern need to be specified. The fabric may be plain dyed, colour woven, printed or embroidered and these ideas are developed primarily by fashion or textile designers. Fabric technologists can be involved in sourcing appropriate companies to design the surface pattern and recommending which printing or dyeing techniques should be used to achieve the look required by a designer or buyer, whilst meeting the retailer's quality standards. Prints can be sourced from:

- fabric manufacturers' ranges;
- retailers' or manufacturers' own design teams;
- freelance print designers or agents;
- trade fairs, e.g. *Indigo* (see Table 6.1).

The most straightforward method of sourcing a printed fabric is to select a print from a fabric manufacturer's own range so they can supply finished, printed cloth in this design. The potential drawback is that this print will also be available to the fabric manufacturer's other customers and may therefore not be exclusive, enabling a retailer's competitors to stock garments in an identical print. The fabric technologist or buyer can sometimes negotiate for a print to be 'confined' to the retailer for a particular season, so that no other stores can sell it at the same time. Prints are usually offered in several colourways and can be printed in the retailer's own colour palette for large orders. If a sample garment is needed with the correct print on it, a length of fabric can be printed from a CAD program using a digital printer much more quickly and cheaply than bulk printing. Fabric technologists assess the quality of printed fabrics by inspecting aesthetic and performance aspects such as print registration, i.e. the correct location of each colour within a print. Finishing removes any excess dye and fixes the colour of fabrics. Additional mechanical or chemical finishing processes can be used to change the appearance or properties of fabrics.

Global fabric sourcing

Clothing manufacturers can make garments from fabric sourced in the same country or import it from various other countries. Most UK garment manufacturers are likely to import the majority of their cloth. Country of origin labels in garments refer only to the location of the clothing manufacturer and not the fabric source. A wide variety of fabrics are available from the Far East. China is renowned for its silk fabrics but virtually all types of natural and synthetic fibres are now available there. Japan is a leading innovator in synthetic fabrics such as polyester and polyamide. European mills continue to manufacture and print knitted and woven fabrics, though these are now relatively expensive, tending to restrict them to the middle and upper levels of the fashion market. Large-scale fabric production in the UK is limited mainly to traditional woollen cloth, e.g. worsted and tweed, woven in the North West and Scotland, and jersey fabric knitted in the East Midlands. UK-based printers usually import most of the fabric they use. It is important that fabrics are sourced within a realistic price bracket for the retailer and in some cases fabric technologists can participate in negotiating fabric prices with manufacturers.

FABRIC DEVELOPMENT

Fabric technologists are likely to work in conjunction with buyers or designers to develop fabrics with suppliers. This means adapting existing fabrics to achieve the combination of properties required to meet the retailers' needs by changing certain elements, e.g. by applying a new finish to a supplier's fabric, such as brushing. The fabric manufacturer may have offered this type of finish on a different fabric in its range and the buyer may have decided to apply it to a fabric to give a soft handle to its garments, to gain an advantage over competitors' products. The buyer can describe the type of fabric required, often using garments bought on directional shopping trips as examples, and the fabric technologist can then liaise with the appropriate supplier to develop samples of the fabric.

Some fabric technologists specialise in fabric development more than the testing and approval aspects of the role. When developing products for a new season, buyers for mass market retailers mainly source fabrics with subtle changes from the previous season's merchandise. This often involves mainly using the same basecloths as in past seasons in new colours and prints combined with the occasional introduction of more innovative fabric constructions and fibre blends. New fabric developments used by high street retailers are often influenced by those used in ready-to-wear collections. It is almost impossible to locate the original manufacturer of a fabric from a bought sample. Fabric technologists or buyers can contact fabric manufacturers with the technical capabilities to make the fabric and send them swatches from a bought sample to see whether they produce anything similar or if they are willing to develop it. As fabric development is a costly exercise this may need to be backed by the promise of a large order from the garment manufacturer supplying the goods to the retailer. The fabric may later become part of the fabric manufacturer's range and be offered to other customers.

The textile industry has been more innovative in technical developments than the clothing industry in recent years. These developments are likely to continue within European and US fabric suppliers to give them a point of difference to overseas competitors with whom they can no longer compete on price. Major innovations have taken place in so-called technical fabrics which have been developed for their functional properties and performance in fields such as sportswear and uniforms.

Synthetic fabrics with environmentally-friendly characteristics are now available as well as fabrics manufactured from organic natural fibres, reflecting the changing priorities of consumers. Innovative synthetic fabrics developed in recent years include:

- Tencel® from Lenzing, which can be recycled and is biodegradable (generic name Lyocell);
- Goretex®, which has micropores allowing perspiration to escape whilst resisting rain;
- Coolmax® from Invista, made from specially engineered polyester fibres, with thermoregulatory and moisture management properties.

Fabric manufacturers have developed micro-encapsulation which allows additional elements to be encapsulated within fibres incorporating scents or insect-repellent finishes. Lingerie brands have designed garment ranges made from fabrics containing micro-encapsulated aromas. Smart fabrics which can respond to the wearer's environment are also under development. Philips is in the process of developing 'wearable electronics' with garments containing mobile phones and cameras to locate the wearer, electronic clubwear and sportswear with MP3 technology to monitor sporting performance. All of these developments are aimed at specific end uses and it is likely that fabric technologists will push the boundaries further by applying similar innovations into fashion fabrics.

CAREER ROUTES

As with most careers in fashion and textiles, fabric technologists can begin their careers at assistant or trainee level. After approximately three years it may be possible to become a fabric technologist responsible for a product area supported by an assistant. Senior fabric technologists usually manage a team of staff and oversee more than one product area. The next level is to be manager or director of the technology department within a supplier, retailer or testing company, which can involve managing garment technologists as well as fabric technologists. Most companies require fabric technologists to have specialist qualifications or experience due to the technical knowledge required for the role, but some consider applicants from textile design courses who demonstrate an aptitude and interest in fabric technology. In the UK, BA (Hons) Textile Technology can be studied at the University of Manchester, Manchester Metropolitan University or the University of Bolton, and other textiles-related courses offer the subject as part of the curriculum.

CASE STUDY

Fabric technologist for a garment supplier

Career path

Ruth Kelly has been a senior fabric technologist since 2003 for clothing manufacturer Crystal Martin International Ltd, located at their head office in Nottinghamshire (see Fig. 6.3). After graduating in 1990 with a BSc (Hons) in Textile Technology, Ruth started work as a development fabric technologist for UK-based

Fig. 6.3 Ruth Kelly at the Crystal Martin International Head Office

lingerie and swimwear manufacturer Columbus Textiles, dealing with products for Marks & Spencer, Nike and Reebok. After four years Ruth moved to a competing underwear and nightwear manufacturer, Corah Garments, as a fabric technologist. In 1996 Ruth planned to take a 'gap year' in Asia but after five months of travelling decided instead to take a job based in Hong Kong as fabric technical manager for Courtaulds Clothing, an outerwear manufacturer. She worked there for four years, managing a team of seven technologists developing products for Marks & Spencer. In 2001 Ruth became a fabric technical manager in Sri Lanka for the underwear division of UK-based Quantum Clothing Ltd before returning to the UK in her current position.

Role and responsibilities

Ruth's product area is bras and lingerie collections for a major UK high street retailer. She works alongside other specialists on the same product including designers, garment technologists, merchandisers and a commercial executive (see Fig. 6.4).

The major elements of her role are:

- ensuring that the designs selected by the customer meet the required quality standards and conform to environmental standards;
- helping to ensure the products are cost-effective and profitable whilst performing adequately;
- developing new fabric ideas;
- helping the product meet the customer's aesthetic requirements;
- sourcing fastenings and trims.

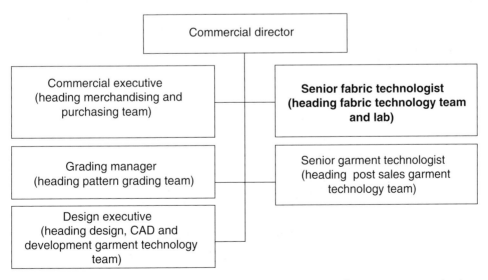

Fig. 6.4 Bras and lingerie collection department structure at Crystal Martin International Ltd

To achieve these objectives, Ruth stresses the importance of teamwork:

It's very important as you couldn't work without the team. If people aren't there, if they're away on a trip for example, you cover and colleagues do the same for you. We're all aiming for the same end result. The designer looks at the aesthetics and the technologist makes sure you can boil wash it and it will still look good!

Ruth visits London once a fortnight for meetings with the retailer and to go comparative shopping. She also travels abroad on a regular basis to visit factories in Sri Lanka, China, India and Hong Kong, where the products are manufactured. Crystal Martin International Ltd was UK-owned until it was taken over by its Chinese parent company Crystal Group in 2004. Ruth says she enjoys liaising with people from different cultures because 'for example in China and Taiwan there are subtle differences in the way they deal with customers'. Ruth describes the most challenging aspects of her job:

Everyone wants everything cheaper but with more on it, so you need to make a product that makes a profit margin combined with good performance. It's difficult to be creative to develop the product and you have to find different ways to bring the price down. There will always be conflict between people in whatever company you work for but you can turn that around. I went on a training course at work on the psychology behind why people behave as they do, which was useful.

Ruth has attended various other training courses within her job on subjects such as information technology and assertiveness.

Career advice

To work effectively as a fabric technologist, Ruth says 'you've got to be able to handle pressure and respond quickly to a situation by focusing and prioritising'. Administration and organisational skills are also important, in order to keep the relevant paperwork up-to-date. Ruth found her first job by chance as she did not know that working for a clothing supplier was an option available to her, and she initially considered becoming a buyer. She offers the following advice to anyone wanting to work as a technologist for a garment manufacturer:

You can make a fabric technologist's job as creative as you want it to be and push the boundaries technically. We look at ranges of fabric with the designers at the fabric mills and get involved in price negotiations, so we're not just looking at technical processes. When I'm employing graduates I look for people who are self-motivated, enthusiastic and can work in a team. It doesn't matter if someone doesn't understand everything technically as long as they are bright and eager to learn, with a good sense of humour. It's an interesting job if you enjoy working with people and being hands-on.

If you want to become a fabric technologist, try to get experience of anything you can that relates to textiles, like visiting garment or fabric manufacturers. Try to learn a language – ideally the same language as the major area where the company does business. If you are able to speak and write Mandarin the opportunities are endless in textiles.

Don't be put off by negative press regarding the industry. It has undergone a major transformation in the last ten years with manufacturing moving increasingly offshore, but there will always be the need for designers, buyers, technologists, merchandisers etc. in the UK, and that has reached a level that I believe will be sustained in the near future. Also it's a fabulous way to travel the world and work offshore.

FURTHER READING

Books

Brackenbury, T. (1992) *Knitted Clothing Technology*. Blackwell Science, Oxford.
Braddock, S. and O'Mahony, M. (2005) *Techno Textiles: Revolutionary Fabrics for Fashion and Design*. No. 2 Thames & Hudson, London.
Cresswell, L. (2001) *Textiles at the Cutting Edge*. Forbes Publications, London.
Taylor, M.A. (1991) *Technology of Textile Properties*. Forbes Publications, London.

Journals

The Journal of the Textile Institute

Websites

www.dti.gov.uk/support/textiles/technical.htm
www.elearning-textiles.co.uk
www.indigo-salon.com
www.interstoff.messefrankfurt.com
www.intertek-labtest.com
www.texworld.messefrankfurt.com

The Textile Institute
1st Floor,
St James's Buildings,
Oxford Street,
Manchester,
M1 6FQ.
0161 2371188
texi.org

Garment technology 7

Fig. 7.1 Liaison between garment technologists and other roles

Garment technologists ensure that sample and production garments achieve the quality standards required by the retailer which will sell those products. Most UK-based garment technologists are employed by suppliers, as manufacturers are required to implement quality procedures by the retailers whom they supply. Many fashion retailers employ in-house garment technologists to liaise with their counterparts in the supply chain, often combining this with the fabric technologist's role (see Chapter 6). Larger retailers tend to keep the two roles separate, because each requires a large amount of specific technical know-how and experience. The term 'garment technology' is being used increasingly to replace the traditional terms 'quality control' (QC) and 'quality assurance' (QA), recognising that this role requires a thorough technical knowledge of garment construction and manufacturing processes. 'Product developer' is another popular job title for a role which combines elements of both garment technology and fashion design. Product developers can be involved in sourcing new ideas for methods of manufacture, fabrics and components.

A garment technologist usually works on a specific product area, e.g. men's tailoring. The garment technologist is usually responsible for:

- garment fittings;
- approval of sealing samples prior to production;
- size and manufacture specifications;
- checking the quality of bulk production;
- monitoring test results;
- product safety, risk analysis and legal requirements;
- wearer trials.

As well as these responsibilities, retail garment technologists present reviews of quality issues in relation to specific products and suppliers each season. Within a manufacturer the garment technologist may also be involved in:

- pattern cutting and grading (see Chapter 5);
- lay planning;
- compiling specification sheets;
- garment costings.

Due to the technical knowledge required in this role, many garment technologists transfer from working for manufacturers to retailers and *vice versa*.

GARMENT FITTINGS

Fitting sessions for suppliers' sample garments are usually arranged by garment technologists in conjunction with retail buyers and mostly take place at the retailer's head office. They may also be attended by garment technologists, product developers, designers and pattern cutters from the supplier. If a representative from the supplier is unable to attend, the retail garment technologist is responsible for forwarding fitting comments to the manufacturer in the form of written notes, sometimes supported by explanatory sketches. Computer software for this purpose uses digital images to show problems with fit or specific style features that need amending to increase the speed and accuracy of alterations.

If a retail garment technologist is visiting a supplier's office or factory, garment fittings can be carried out there. When sample garments are produced they may initially be tried on mannequins in the supplier's design room. Padded mannequins can be bought to either a standard size or to the specific dimensions used by a particular retailer. It is essential to try a sample which will go into bulk production on a live model to ensure that a person can get into the garment and move around comfortably. Usually models are hired on a regular basis from an agency or some companies may employ house models and it is important to try to use the same person consistently or someone with very similar measurements (usually size 12 for womenswear, size 42 for menswear and age 7/8 for childrenswear). Members of staff of the right size may occasionally be requested to try on garments if the model is not available and a sample needs to be looked at urgently.

Amendments can be made to a sample worn by the model using pins and a tape measure. Changes are often made to the fit of first samples by the retailer. The supplier's fashion designer, pattern cutter or garment technologist may be responsible for amending patterns and arranging for a second sample to be made if required. Garments are usually approved for production after first or second samples have been submitted to the retailer, but for new or particularly complex styles further samples may be requested. Buyers and designers can be responsible for making decisions about the aesthetic aspects of garment fitting, such as silhouette, length and proportion, whilst garment technologists look at the samples mainly from a technical perspective.

APPROVAL OF SEALING SAMPLES PRIOR TO PRODUCTION

When the fit of a style has been approved, the supplier is usually asked to send two identical samples to the retailer. The garment technologist signs and attaches a 'seal' to these garments, which are of the quality standard expected in production (see Fig. 7.2). The retailer keeps one of the 'sealing samples' (or 'sealers') for reference and the other is returned to the supplier before patterns for this style are produced in the complete size range. Retailers such as Marks & Spencer, for whom quality standards are a priority, request sealing samples at various stages of product development and bulk production. However, this increases costs and

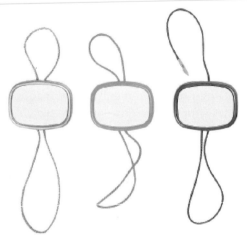

Fig. 7.2 Sample seals
Courtesy of Morplan

although quality control is improved, fashionability can suffer due to the additional time required for these extra approvals. Seals of different colours can be used for sealing samples to represent the different stages, e.g. green seals may identify samples in the smallest and largest sizes. In some cases, suppliers are given responsibility for sealing bulk production garments.

SIZE SPECIFICATIONS

Once the sealing sample of a style has been approved, the retail garment technologist can compile a size specification or request one from the supplier. Each retailer has its own set of sizing rules (see Chapter 5). Within a clothing supplier the garment technologist, pattern cutter or grader may be responsible for making production patterns in the full range of sizes. The size specification is a table of measurements for various parts of an item of clothing in several different garment sizes. This can be compiled manually or by using appropriate computer software.

CHECKING THE QUALITY OF BULK PRODUCTION

Most fashion retailers supply their own quality manuals to manufacturers to ensure that the standards they require for their products are crystal clear to both parties. Retail garment technologists may be responsible for writing, reviewing or updating the company's quality manuals, taking into account changes in the law or the market at which the products are aimed. Quality manuals cover legislation, health and safety issues and environmental considerations. With the increase in overseas sourcing quality manuals may be adapted to reflect the working practices in different countries and to ensure clear communication. Indications of poor standards which garment technologists watch out for when inspecting garments include:

- puckered or inconsistent stitching quality;
- seam slippage (i.e. seams which come apart easily);
- security of fastenings and trims;
- position of pockets or fastenings;
- loose threads.

Garment technologists working for suppliers are responsible for checking the quality standards of garments during production and sending samples of these garments to the retailer if required. Fabric testing is part of the quality control process for fashion retailers. Checking that the testing standards for fabrics have been met by the supplier is part of the retail garment technologist's role – or the fabric technologist's, if the company has one (see Chapter 5).

Retail garment technologists sometimes travel to visit suppliers to observe garments being manufactured. These visits are known as an 'in-work checks' and

Fig. 7.3 Garment inspection in a clothing factory
Courtesy of Intertek-Labtest

involve assessing the quality standards of products which are currently being manufactured or are ready for delivery. This can help to save the time and expense of returning low-quality merchandise to the manufacturer if the garments are rejected. Quality inspections include measuring various dimensions of garments to ensure that they meet the required specifications and assessing the quality of manufacture. As fabric is a flexible material a slight variation of 0.5 cm to 1 cm from the specified measurement is allowed depending upon the part of the garment, referred to as 'tolerance'. It is impossible for retail garment technologists to see all of the styles for which they are responsible in production, particularly as so many are manufactured overseas. This has led to an increase in self-certification by suppliers, working to a specified inspection system, giving them more responsibility for adhering to the retailer's quality standards in production. Independent testing labs can also be contracted to carry out in-work checks on behalf of the retailer (see Fig. 7.3).

Finished garments are transported to the retailer's distribution centre (DC), which is often based in one central location or several regional sites. Retail garment technologists often travel to the DC to check the quality of stock prior to its delivery to stores. Retailers often employ QCs based permanently at the DC who liaise with the garment technology department at head office. QCs inspect a small percentage of garments at random. If a quality problem is anticipated, some styles may require 100 per cent inspection at the warehouse and if the quality is consistently low, the delivery could be rejected.

PRODUCT SAFETY, RISK ANALYSIS AND LEGAL REQUIREMENTS

Retailers need to comply with the minimum British Standards health and safety regulations and may have their own additional safety requirements. Retailers with rigorous quality procedures request their suppliers to carry out 'risk analysis' for every style, which involves analysing every aspect of the garment to anticipate any quality problems which could occur during production. Childrenswear quality standards are particularly stringent to ensure that children are not endangered by wearing garments. Consequently, there are legal restrictions and product safety guidelines on the use of drawcords in hoods and some retailers require their manufacturers to use metal detectors on all childrenswear and lingerie products, to ensure no pins or needles have been inadvertently attached to garments.

Consumer legislation requires the fibre composition and washing instructions to be labelled in all garments and nightwear fabrics must be tested for flammability. Retail garment technologists are usually responsible for checking that fabric and garment testing has taken place and for specifying washcare instructions. They also decide on the location of the labels within the garments and communicate this to their suppliers. Labels stating the retailer or brand and garment size are conventionally located in the centre back inside neck or waist and a side seam label usually includes washing instructions, fibre content and barcode. Some labels include the country of origin, if it is company policy to do so, but this is no longer a legal requirement in the UK.

PRODUCT DATA MANAGEMENT

Product data management (PDM) systems are computer programs for the compilation of information about garments throughout product development and production processes. PDM is particularly relevant to garment technologists, although designers, pattern cutters, buyers and merchandisers may also use it. A web-based PDM system enables retailers and suppliers to participate in 'e-collaboration' by allowing them access through a security code to view and update the progress of garments. The product data can include drawings, costings, size specifications and other relevant documents. PDM systems can be compatible with other software such as CAD/CAM to allow design and pattern-cutting information to be integrated within them.

SUPPLIER AUDITS

Retail garment technologists are responsible for auditing new and existing suppliers, which can also involve their colleagues in buying and fabric technology. The results of the audit allow the retailer to decide whether to begin or continue working with a particular supplier. This is often carried out by retail garment technologists at a senior or management level by visiting the factory concerned and inspecting various criteria which may include:

- consistency of quality;
- standards of service;
- design and technical facilities;
- machinery available and process systems;

- speed of delivery;
- ethical issues;
- health and safety code of practice;
- employment of young workers;
- human rights.

WEARER TRIALS

Wearer trials are usually conducted by garment technologists at the early stages of approval if there is thought to be a potential quality problem with a product, e.g. if fabric test results for tear strength are borderline fails. Sample or bulk garments are worn and washed several times to ensure that the garments are of a satisfactory standard before the bulk production is delivered to stores. The garment technologist distributes the garments to a panel of potential customers who wear and wash the clothes for a specified amount of time and complete questionnaires to record the findings, which are then analysed to see how they have performed. After the wearer trial the garment technologist decides whether or not the products are of an adequate standard to be sold in store and the buyer may be consulted when this decision is made.

CAREER ROUTES

Junior positions for garment technologists are available for graduates at assistant or trainee level. It was once the norm for garment technologists or QCs to begin their careers as clothing factory machinists, without any formal fashion or textiles education. This route is becoming increasingly rare in the UK due to the movement of garment production offshore, resulting in a limited amount of people with direct experience of clothing manufacture. Experience within manufacturing is likely to be viewed as an asset when applying for a garment technologist's role for a fashion retailer. Sizeable numbers of machinists used to be employed in the UK clothing industry but machining is a low-paid job with little prospect of promotion and with the advent of the minimum wage and high imports, this is not viewed as an attractive job for many young people.

Working at assistant level usually involves shadowing a garment technologist and helping with everyday tasks, focusing mainly on garment inspection and checking test results. An assistant may be promoted to garment technologist after two or more years experience, and could then become responsible for a complete product area and visit offshore manufacturers. A senior garment technologist or QA manager oversees other garment technologists, is responsible for contributing to the company's quality strategy and often liaises with other managers within the business. A garment technology (or QA) manager is generally the highest level in this field within retail. Large clothing suppliers may offer opportunities for QA managers to progress to become production directors.

There are various technically-orientated courses from which a high proportion of graduates become garment technologists, such as BA (Hons) Fashion and Textile Management at Nottingham Trent University, BA (Hons) Clothing Design with Technology at Manchester Metropolitan University and BA (Hons) Product Design and Development for Clothing at the London College of Fashion. Many fashion design graduates become garment technologists, usually after several years of experience in designing for clothing suppliers.

CASE STUDY

Garment technologist for a childrenswear retailer

Career path

Sarah Jones* is a senior garment technologist in the boyswear department at Adams' head office in Nuneaton, Warwickshire. After completing a BTEC Higher National Diploma in Fashion and Textiles she became a pattern cutter in her first job. She then worked as a garment technologist for a jersey and knitwear manufacturer for five years. Sarah transferred from garment manufacture into fashion retail as a garment technologist for the George clothing range before joining Adams in 2001.

Roles and responsibilities

Sarah is in charge of product development and approval on the toddler boys and footwear departments. She is also responsible for the strategy of the whole QA team at Adams which involves:

- managing the QA team (see Fig. 7.4);
- controlling budgets;
- decision making and problem solving;
- visiting garment and footwear suppliers;
- carrying out factory audits.

Sarah spends much of her time liaising with suppliers of garments, footwear and components to maintain the quality standards of the product range. Within Adams' head office she works closely with buyers, designers, merchandisers and the packaging department. Sarah has to work on several ranges of merchandise at once as she explains:

In October we are working on product development for the following spring/summer season. Products with a long lead time have been finalised and approved for phases one and two of spring/summer. We are focusing now on products for phases one

*The interviewee's name has been changed.

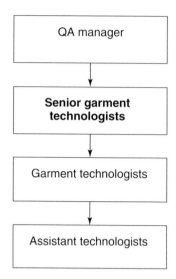

Fig. 7.4 The structure of the QA team at Adams

and two with shorter lead times and products for phase three, which is sold in high summer.

Since most of the garments are manufactured offshore, Sarah needs to travel in her job:

Most of the travelling is overseas as our products are manufactured in lots of locations including China, Sri Lanka, India, Turkey, Morocco and Romania. The most unglamorous part of my job is visiting factories and it can be hard work in some countries with communication issues. We also visit UK suppliers, though there are not that many now. We go to UK offices of suppliers to do fittings etc. as well as store visits to our stores and the competition.

Sarah particularly enjoys working with suppliers, developing products and problem solving within her role. She has had training courses at work in presentation skills, negotiation skills and other managerial subjects, but her technical knowledge has been learnt within the job. Sarah explains some of the skills which are relevant to her role:

Teamwork is extremely important as we do it all the time. It is imperative that your team is informed of decisions and we are all responsible for the product. It's also necessary to be enthusiastic and pro-active.

Career advice

When employing garment technologists within her team Sarah says she looks for 'talented individuals with the relevant experience who want to succeed'. She gives the following advice for those considering a career in garment technology:

It's hard work and can be frustrating when dealing with suppliers so you need to keep a sense of humour and have tenacity!

FURTHER READING

Books

Cooklin, G. (1997) *Garment Technology for Fashion Designers.* Blackwell Publishing, Oxford.
Tyler, D. (2000) *Carr and Latham's Technology of Clothing Manufacture.* Third edition. Blackwell Publishing, Oxford.
Von, E. (2004) *Clothing Technology.* Verlag Europa-Lehrmittel, Nourney.

Magazines

International Journal of Clothing Science and Technology

Websites

www.bsi-global.com
www.gerbertechnology.com
www.morplan.com

Sales and marketing in the fashion and textiles industry

Fig. 8.1 Liaison between sales roles and other roles within the fashion and textiles industry

Sales and marketing roles in the fashion and textiles industry involve selling and promoting products to retailers, brands or suppliers. The sales jobs described in this chapter were traditionally referred to as sales representatives, but 'sales executive' has become one of the most popular terms in current use, entailing business-to-business liaison within the trade. Sales executives can be employees of manufacturers, suppliers, brands or wholesalers or can operate as agents. Most sales roles within fashion and textiles involve:

- liaising with customers' buyers, designers, merchandisers and technologists;
- liaising with designers, merchandisers and technologists within the company by whom they are employed;

- presenting fabric or garment ranges at meetings and trade fairs;
- increasing or maintaining sales.

Sales representatives can be partly office-based but usually travel extensively to see customers and to visit the companies whose ranges they sell.

Marketing positions within fashion and textiles can be based in-house or a company can employ a marketing agency to cover this area. Medium to large companies often have their own marketing departments and in smaller businesses responsibility for marketing may be subsumed within the sales department. Marketing teams are responsible for promoting products or services from business-to-business in the case of suppliers, from business-to-consumer within retailers and a combination of both when working for fashion brands.

Fig. 8.2 Liaison between marketing roles and other roles within the fashion and textiles industry

SALES AGENTS WITHIN THE FASHION AND TEXTILES INDUSTRY

Within the fashion and textiles industry it is common practice for sales agents to be appointed to sell products on behalf of a company. Sales agents may be self-employed, working on an individual basis (see Chapter 17) or as part of a team within a sales agency. In both cases, sales agents are usually paid entirely on a commission basis, receiving a percentage of the turnover for the amount of products they sell. Agents therefore have a high incentive to achieve sales targets and it is preferable for them to sell product ranges from more than one company rather than rely on a single source of income. It is usual for ranges sold by the same agent to be compatible whilst not competing directly with each other.

Sales agents normally sell products from fabric manufacturers or clothing brands and are responsible for selling within a particular region or country. The terms 'marketing agency' or 'fashion agency' are used for sales agencies selling a selection of fashion brands. London-based Four Marketing is an example of a fashion agency distributing primarily menswear brands comprising Stone Island, CP Company, Fake London, Evisu and Raf Simons. Like many agencies, Four Marketing have a showroom in which they can conduct business meetings with customers with access to samples from garment ranges. Showrooms often have the appearance of retail outlets but are only open to trade customers by appointment. In London the showrooms of many fashion brands are concentrated around the Great Portland Street area in the West End and around Shoreditch in the East End.

SALES ROLES IN THE TEXTILES INDUSTRY

Fabric mills and printing companies usually appoint sales agents in various countries to sell their ranges to garment manufacturers, brands, retailers and designers. Fabric ranges are shown in the form of swatches on hangers (called headers). Sales agents arrange meetings with buyers, designers or fabric technologists at customers' offices, agents' offices or trade fairs to present fabric ranges. Sales agents make appointments through existing contacts or advertising in trade magazines, websites or directories of trade fairs at which they exhibit. Customers request headers or lengths of fabric from which sample garments can be made (see Chapter 6). Sales agents also provide information to customers regarding:

- production and delivery lead times;
- price per metre;
- fabric width;
- fibre composition;
- construction, quality and washcare instructions;
- minimum order quantities.

Headers and samples are sent to the customers free of charge or at a nominal price. Fabric sampling incurs large costs to fabric manufacturers but is accepted as the primary method of promoting a company's products. For this reason, fabric companies are understandably reluctant to offer headers and sample lengths to those who are unlikely to be able to order from them, such as students and relatively small companies. As it would be uneconomical to keep large quantities of cloth in stock and customers often have their own specific design requirements, fabric is made or printed specially for a customer's bulk order. To make bulk manufacture financially viable, the sales agent specifies a minimum order quantity which may vary from 300 to 3000 metres.

Agents usually quote list prices for fabrics and these can be negotiable when an order is placed. Fabric prices may or may not include delivery and the sales agent should clarify whether the price per metre quoted is:

- ex-mill;
- FOB (free on board);
- CIF (including carriage, insurance and freight).

Ex-mill prices mean that no transport is included whereas an FOB price includes delivery to a port near the fabric manufacturer, from which the customer then needs to arrange and pay for shipping and insurance. A CIF fabric price is more realistic as it includes transport to the garment manufacturer or a port nearby and insurance during the journey, but can be quoted only if the customer knows the anticipated destination of the fabric.

MERCHANTS AND WHOLESALERS

Fabric merchants import bulk quantities of fabric into the UK from fabric manufacturers to keep in stock in a warehouse. This provides a valuable service to European manufacturers supplying fast fashion retailers as the fabric is immediately available, cutting out the time it would take to wait for production and shipping. However, the disadvantages are that the selection of fabrics is limited and the fabrics are more expensive than buying them direct because the merchant needs to make a profit. Buying fabric from a merchant is also useful for designers or manufacturers who make relatively small amounts of garments as there is usually no minimum order quantity. Fabric merchants require the same sales skills as agents and also operate as fabric buyers in effect, requiring the commercial foresight to foresee their customers' requirements. Wholesalers function in a similar way to merchants in that they are 'middle-men' stocking products which they have bought from manufacturers to sell to retailers. Many fashion brands and ready-to-wear designers work on a wholesale system, employing sales representatives or agents to sell their garments. Individual independent stores or small chains invariably buy from wholesalers as the quantities they purchase are generally too small to meet manufacturers' minimum quantities.

SELLING FASHION BRANDS AND READY-TO-WEAR RANGES

Fashion brands specialise in design development and sales of product ranges and contract out garment manufacture to clothing suppliers. In addition to selling their products on a wholesale basis to retailers, contemporary casualwear brands Boxfresh and Firetrap amongst others also have some of their own retail outlets. This gives them the opportunity to sell the complete product range together (as opposed to a limited selection) and these stores become part of the brand's promotional strategy.

Many sportswear brands have been adopted as fashion items. Branded ranges have always been popular in the lingerie sector and high quality fashion brands with relatively classic styling dominate mainstream middle market womenswear such as Libra, aimed primarily at the occasion wear market. Most brands exhibit their ranges at international trade fairs to present their collections to new and existing customers. Ready-to-wear designer collections can be sold at exhibitions which run concurrently with the runway shows. Designers themselves may liaise with buyers if the company is very small or a member of the design team may be responsible for sales in addition to other duties.

SALES ROLES FOR GARMENT SUPPLIERS

Sales executives are usually paid a set salary by the supplier or manufacturer and in some cases may also receive a percentage of sales turnover as an incentive. They generally work exclusively for a supplier, based either at a factory or office located near to the company's major customers. Many fabric and garment suppliers which previously manufactured in the UK have retained their sales and design functions in this country whilst sub-contracting production to companies overseas. Sales executives within some of the larger garment suppliers are known as 'commercial executives', often with broader responsibilities than a sales role, such as managing a department working on a specific product area, and including designers. Sales executives are likely to work on more than one customer's account. They may be responsible for formulating sales strategies which can involve aiming to expand sales by targeting new customers. Usually, sales executives for garment suppliers work on an equal level to their designer colleagues and regularly attend meetings together with retailers. Some UK suppliers work on a CMT basis (cut, make and trim), meaning that they do not offer a design service but simply manufacture the products, with patterns and fabric provided by their customers. The sales role in this type of garment supplier may be combined with managing production or running the business, as the companies are often relatively small with minimal overheads. CMT manufacturers are popular with ready-to-wear designers because some can produce small quantities of garments and they obviously do not require a design service from their suppliers (see Chapter 4).

Offshore suppliers

Clothing manufacturers located overseas sometimes sell their products in the UK through their own sales executives working directly with retailers. Alternatively offshore manufacturers can work with UK-based suppliers sales agents. Many retailers work with their own or independent overseas buying offices, usually staffed with local people who understand the local language, market and culture and communicate well in English. This role is known as a merchandiser, though it differs substantially from that of a merchandiser based at a retailer's head office. The merchandiser is a point of contact for the UK-based buyer who liaises directly with manufacturers' sales executives.

Cost prices

The price paid by a retailer to a garment supplier for a product is known as the cost price, which is a fraction of the final retail selling price paid by consumers in stores. A sales executive for a garment supplier is responsible for submitting cost prices to retailers, consisting of the materials, trims, labour and overheads which contribute to the manufacture of garments plus a percentage for profit. Sales executives aim to gain the highest feasible price for the product and should achieve at least the minimum amount needed to make the sale profitable for the supplier. Conversely, the fashion buyer aims to pay the lowest possible price to maximise the retailer's profit margin, so negotiation is frequently necessary.

Sample and bulk orders

Garment suppliers' sales executives liaise with fashion buyers to inform them of developments while garments are being sampled, often with the support of the supplier's design team. Once a style has been selected for a range the retailer's fashion merchandiser places a purchase order with the supplier and the sales executive deals with the administration of the order. Garment suppliers have minimum order quantities to make orders financially viable. In effect the purchase order is a legally binding contract between the two companies so it is vital that the sales executive confirms information such as the agreed price, quantity and delivery date.

MARKETING ROLES IN FASHION AND TEXTILES

Large fashion retailers and brands often have their own marketing departments or brand managers to organise promotional activities to communicate the company's brand image and values to consumers. This may involve commissioning advertising agencies to produce advertising campaigns. However, advertising is not a widespread promotional technique in the fashion industry, due to the constantly changing nature of fashion products. There are several more subtle and cost-effective ways of promoting fashion ranges to potential consumers which are more popular, such as:

- PR (see Chapter 13);
- fashion shows;
- press launches;
- sponsorship;

- celebrity endorsement;
- point-of-purchase material;
- special offers;
- competitions;
- websites.

Marketing agencies can deal with various aspects of promotion to formulate a marketing strategy for a fashion business and integrated marketing agencies can also provide advertising. Marketing agencies tend to deal with different product types rather than being fashion specialists. Within a marketing agency account managers work with specific retailers or brands. Marketing roles have an emphasis on knowledge of marketing techniques rather than product manufacture.

CAREER ROUTES

There are limited numbers of junior or assistant sales executive positions. Traditionally, selling within the fashion and textiles industry was often a family business. Nowadays, people often move into sales roles having gained relevant experience in other areas of the business such as design, buying or merchandising. Selling fashion and textiles from business-to-business can potentially be a highly lucrative career as many such jobs are paid on sales results. However, there is an inherent risk that sales, and therefore income, can drop so this is a field for those who are highly motivated to achieve results. It is not essential for sales executives to have fashion or textiles-related qualifications. However, a degree in a relevant subject such as fashion and textile management or fashion marketing could be advantageous when applying for this type of job. A marketing or business qualification can obviously be useful for those working in marketing departments or agencies.

CASE STUDIES

Sales manager for a wholesale fabric collection

Career path

Carolyn Chapman has been sales manager for the Liberty Fabric wholesale collection since 1999. She studied fashion design and says she 'migrated into textiles accidentally' after graduating in the early 1990s. At the time design jobs were scarce and she was offered her first position working for a small retail fabric company. From there she pursued her career in textiles, working in wholesale sales administration to learn more about the practicalities of wholesale selling, then moving into fabric production roles to find out more about the technical aspects of weaving and printing.

Role and responsibilities

Liberty Fabric (a sister company to the Liberty store in London) is a design-led wholesale fabric company supplying designers and clothing manufacturers worldwide. Carolyn is responsible for managing their sales of wholesale fabric (see Fig. 8.3). This consists of two seasonal fabric collections per year (spring/summer and autumn/winter) launched in January and September respectively, which are designed in-house. All of their designs are shown and sold on fabric to companies for use in garment collections. Carolyn manages a sales team of six people and is the primary contact for international sales agents. Her main responsibilities are:

- marketing, promoting and presenting the fabric collection;
- devising sales presentations;
- ensuring that profitable sales are achieved;
- managing and developing key accounts;
- identifying new sales and product opportunities;
- writing the seasonal press release, range notes and sales brief;
- exhibiting the fabric collection at European trade shows;
- ensuring that the key design messages behind the collection are conveyed to the sales team, international agents, trade press and customers.

In addition, Carolyn says:

A design background has been invaluable in my current role. Knowledge of fashion design, pattern cutting and garment construction helps me enormously to understand what customers look for when building a clothing collection and selecting fabric. One of my main focuses at Liberty Fabric has been to promote the individuality of the wholesale fabric design process and the unique way the design studio here develop colour and design concepts from personal research and inspiration complemented by historical research in the Liberty Fabric archive.

Fig. 8.3 Promotional postcard for Liberty Fabric range A/W 2007
All designs are copyright of Liberty plc

The fabric collection is launched to wholesale customers 12 months ahead of the time when it will be sold as finished garments in stores. This allows our customers approximately six months to design and develop garment shapes and styles before showing their collections at catwalk events, selling to store buyers or presenting to merchandisers and buyers for range selection.

Carolyn liaises daily with the other departments in Liberty Fabric and works particularly closely with the design and production teams. Here she explains the practicalities of selling the fabric range:

Our fabric collection is displayed on headers and arranged into themes, which we explain in our sales presentations. We also use colour and design 'mood' boards to help explain colour and print direction for the season. International sales agents present the range to customers in their local territory, identifying sales opportunities and providing a sales communication service. We work directly with customers in the UK, presenting the fabric collection from our showroom at Regent Street or travelling to customers' offices throughout the UK. Exhibiting the collection at trade shows like Première Vision gives us the opportunity to target many customers in one location. We aim to make our range as diverse as possible to appeal to all our customer types. However, we do think of which customers might be interested in a particular design 'look' when we are selecting designs and colourways for the collection. My design background has also enabled me to change how we present the collection and, as a result, we have forged stronger relationships with existing customers and attracted a new generation of Liberty Fabric customers.

Carolyn describes the most enjoyable features of her job:

I like the freedom to identify new opportunities and develop ideas to inspire and enthuse customers. I've always had a particular love of fabrics, the various properties they have and how different fabrics create different effects when made into garments, complementing and challenging these properties. And I've always loved Liberty Fabric. I've also always been interested in trends and forecasting and Liberty Fabric now present their own trend preview presentation each season, focusing on defined colour palettes and print direction. It's great to be able to incorporate projects that are of personal interest to me into my current role.

Career advice

Carolyn points out that there are various routes to a career in fabric sales:

In my first job the focus was very much on 'practical' selling: unrolling fabrics, showing colour and fabric combinations together, offering advice on design, pattern cutting and construction. It was great hands-on experience that provided me with the best grounding for where I am now. The overall advice I can give would be that there is no right or wrong route providing it is fulfilling to you personally – challenging, motivating, stimulating. Everyone you speak with will be able to tell you their own personal experiences and each will be different. Find what motivates you – your own strengths and weak-

nesses, challenges, loves and dislikes – and what feels right. It's your chance to follow your own path and create your own experiences.

Sales manager for a clothing manufacturer

Career path

Deborah Turner has been employed since 2002 as a sales manager for jeans and casualwear manufacturer Fashionwear, a company supplying high street fashion multiples (see Fig. 8.4). She graduated with a BA (Hons) in Fashion Design in 1985 and started her first job as a trainee buyer for menswear at Next the same year. She progressed within the company to become a buyer, then senior buyer. Deborah then transferred from fashion retailing to manufacturing when she took on the role of brand manager for Viyella shirts in 1994. Her next career move was as a university lecturer in fashion buying and marketing in 1999 before going back into the industry in her current role.

Role and responsibilities

In addition to Deborah's responsibility for sales, she is also involved in the product development process. Because of this, she has a pattern cutter and sample machinists within her team. Deborah has adapted her job to reflect her skills, and her knowledge of fashion design and buying are a great advantage to her when dealing with retailers.

Fig. 8.4 Deborah Turner, sales manager for Fashionwear

Deborah's main responsibilities are to generate sales from retailers and her pay is performance-related. She fulfils these orders by liaising with colleagues at Fashionwear's Leicester-based head office, where all of the administration, garment washing, finishing, packing and quality control take place. Fashionwear produced garments at this site until 2003 when, like many UK-based clothing suppliers, they moved production offshore. Deborah describes the responsibilities of her job as:

- initiating marketing strategies to deliver agreed sales with the company owners;
- putting designs from customers into work, identifying price points and resolving any production issues to satisfy the customer's needs;
- sourcing fabrics and trims which can achieve customers' price points and quality performance standards;
- calculating cost prices and negotiating agreed prices with the customer;
- fitting development samples through to 'gold seals' with the customer, ensuring that subsequent fit samples are adjusted accordingly;
- ensuring that orders obtained from the customer are commercially viable for production;
- ensuring that bulk trims are agreed with the customer and are correct before application to the goods;
- ensuring that bulk fabrics adhere to the customers' test performance standards before delivery;
- ensuring that the customer is kept up to date with the progress of orders;
- liaising with the customer on a daily basis and interacting with the buying, merchandise, design, fabric and garment technology departments.

Deborah travels to Paris twice a year to source fabrics at *Première Vision* and visits Fashionwear's factory in Tunisia when required. She does comparative shopping within the UK to remain aware of the merchandise on offer in the women's jeans market. She discusses the technical aspects of product development with Fashionwear's garment technologist, who travels to the factory to put the designs into work. She often completes working drawings and specifications for products.

To develop design ideas with retailers, Deborah takes samples of garments, fabrics and trims to her frequent meetings with buyers at Per Una. They discuss developments and prices, working on product details and fit until the buyer approves the garment and it is ready to go into production. She also liaises with Per Una's merchandisers to organise delivery schedules and repeat orders of styles which have been selected. Deborah explains some of the tasks she is involved in at Fashionwear's head office:

I co-ordinate production capacity and delivery dates with the planning manager. I also talk to the machine technician and production manager about the make-up and finishing techniques which can be achieved before garments are made in bulk.

Deborah explains why communication skills are important in her sales role:

I enjoy garment development, creating commercial product that returns high sales and subsequent repeats. But there are many areas during the progress of a garment when issues can arise, you can try to pre-empt some and put in measures to avoid these, but some will be out of your control. It is at these critical points that you must communicate well with the customer if you are to maintain a good relationship with them. We all have sales targets to meet, and if, for example, deliveries are potentially going to go late at least if you give advance warning this gives the customer the ability to move their stock around and perhaps you can negotiate earlier delivery on another item, thus maintaining your output.

Career advice

Deborah encourages interviewees applying for jobs in sales within the fashion and textiles industry to demonstrate enthusiasm and eagerness to learn. 'Self-motivation, communication and organisational skills are priorities in this kind of work' she adds. For those wanting to work in a sales role Deborah also advises:

You have to remember that the customer is always right. Be open and honest when dealing with them and in turn you will gain respect. Be realistic with deadlines and back everything up in writing.

FURTHER READING

Books

Easey, M. (2002) *Fashion Marketing. Second edition.* Blackwell Publishing, Oxford.

Fill, C. and Fill, K. (2005) *Business to Business Marketing – Relationships, Systems and Communications.* FT Prentice-Hall, Harlow.

Jobber, D. and Lancaster, G. (2003) *Selling and Sales Management.* Sixth edition. FT Prentice-Hall, Harlow.

Kotler, P., Saunders, J. Armstrong, G. and Wong, V. (2004) *Principles of Marketing – The European Edition.* Prentice-Hall, London.

Magazines

Drapers

Websites

londonfashionweek.co.uk

Fashion buying

Fig 9.1 Liaison between fashion buyers and other roles

Fashion buyers work for retailers and are responsible for overseeing the selection of a range of products aimed at a specific type of customer and price bracket. The buying role can vary significantly between different companies and market sectors. Buyers of ready-to-wear or branded merchandise select garments from finalised product ranges which are sold to them on a wholesale basis, containing the label of the designer or brand (see Chapter 4). In contrast, buyers of own label ranges develop products in collaboration with their suppliers, which are usually sold under the retailer's label. Many fashion retailers have separate buying departments or divisions – for menswear, womenswear, childrenswear and homeware. In a small company buyers may be responsible for a wide range of product types but in larger multiple retailers responsibility for buying is subdivided into smaller areas such as tailoring or accessories. Buying often involves more extensive travel to a variety of worldwide locations than most other jobs within fashion and textiles, to visit suppliers and research into trends.

BUYING BRANDED AND 'DESIGNER' MERCHANDISE

Most stores which sell products from branded or designer ranges are independent retailers or department stores, e.g. Browns and House of Fraser. Owners or managers of individual independent stores often combine the buying role with selling to customers. Larger independent stores with more than one branch usually employ full-time buyers, such as USC and Republic which have expanded significantly throughout the UK since 2000, reflecting growing consumer demand for fashion brands. The processes and events in which buyers for branded and designer merchandise generally participate for each season or phase (part of a season) are shown in Fig. 9.2. This buying cycle is in constant progression and it is likely that the buyer will be involved in monitoring the delivery and sales figures of one season's collection whilst planning to buy the next season's range.

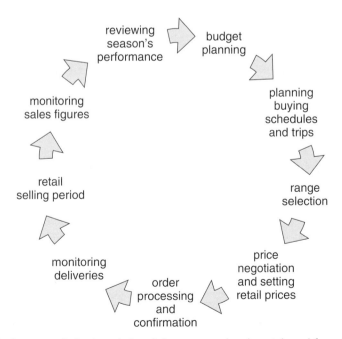

Fig 9.2 The buying cycle for branded and designer merchandise. Adapted from Goworek (2001) p. 129

Buyers select garments from designer and branded ranges mainly through the following methods:

- attending fashion shows;
- visiting showrooms;
- attending trade fairs or exhibitions;
- meetings with sales representatives at the retailer's premises (see Chapter 8).

Designer ranges

Ready-to-wear collections usually bear the designer's name on the label and have runway shows which enhance awareness and the desirability of the range to fashion consumers (see Chapter 4). Buyers of designer ranges may be invited to attend ready-to-wear fashion shows in London, Paris, Milan or New York to view the collections from which they intend to buy. However, buying decisions are more likely to be made before or after the runway shows in the showrooms of the designers or their sales agents (see Chapter 8). *London Fashion Week* also presents an exhibition to give the designers a base to do business with the buyers who attend this event. Having seen a variety of collections, buyers usually then review which products are most suitable for their customers before placing orders.

Branded ranges

Branded ranges retail at similar prices to diffusion ranges in the middle market or compete with the upper end of the mass market (see Chapter 4). Prices of branded ranges are higher than those of many high street multiples. Department stores may sell several brands alongside each other which may be selected by a fashion buyer working for the store. Sales figures for branded merchandise can be influenced by several factors which are controlled by the brand, such as advertising and promotion campaigns and the brand's quality of service and delivery. Buyers can visit relevant trade fairs around the world twice a year to review a range of brands within their market sector (see Table 9.1). Fashion trade fairs are listed in *Drapers* magazine, which also includes reviews of the fairs and regular

Table 9.1 Key fashion trade fairs

Trade fair	Product types	Location	Timing
Pure Womenswear	Contemporary womenswear, accessories and footwear	London	February and August
Pitti Immagine Uomo	Menswear	Florence	January and June
Pitti Immagine Bimbo	Childrenswear	Florence	January and July
Moda UK moda-uk.co.uk	Mainstream womenswear, menswear, footwear and accessories	Birmingham	February and August
London Edge	Alternative fashion and clubwear	London	September

features about fashion brands, aimed at trade customers. Trade fairs are also mentioned in various fashion websites, such as fashionunited.com. UK fashion trade fairs take place twice a year, several being based at Olympia and the NEC, enabling buyers to choose from a selection of international brands without needing to travel overseas (see Chapter 8).

Trade fairs typically take place over a three-day period and several may run concurrently in the same city, allowing buyers to view a variety of fairs in one trip. Exhibitor directories are useful for contacting brands after the show. *Pure Womenswear* is the largest individual fashion trade fair in the UK with over 800 exhibitors. There are also several small shows for niche areas of the market in other locations, such as *Surf Shop* in Exeter. Access to fashion trade fairs is restricted to trade visitors and tickets are available prior to the shows through the venues or exhibition organisers. Groups of students may be permitted to enter some trade shows if an advance booking has been made by their college or university.

BUYING OWN LABEL RANGES

Most fashion multiples sell own label ranges and their buyers are involved in developing these products. The extent of the buyer's involvement in product development can vary depending on the way the retailer's buying department operates and the level of seniority and background of the buyer, e.g. someone qualified in fashion design may have more influence on the design of the products. Those buyers without formal fashion qualifications may rely more on their suppliers for design input. The experienced own label buyer's role involves a wide variety of tasks which are mostly carried out through liaising with colleagues and external suppliers (see Fig. 9.3). Department stores buy a combination of branded and own label merchandise and it is usual for them to develop and sell exclusive own label ranges under a different name to that of the store, such as House of Fraser's Linea ranges of menswear, womenswear and homeware.

Knowledge of sales figures and other information from one season influence the development of retailer's future ranges. Buyers can work on up to three seasons simultaneously, e.g. monitoring sales figures for the current season whilst fitting garments for the next and researching into trends for the following season. A season loosely refers to a six-month selling period from February to July for spring/summer and August to January for autumn/winter. The seasons can be subdivided further into phases of one or two months though some fashion-led retailers such as H&M have new styles delivered on almost a daily basis. In chain stores the buying cycle from initial research through to the delivery of products into stores often used to take up to a year but many retailers are now competing to get 'fast fashion' styles into stores by reducing the timescale within elements of the buying cycle. Inspired by fashion forward companies like Zara and Topshop, which can translate designer looks for the high street within a matter of weeks, Marks & Spencer, renowned for its classic middle mass market clothing, launched a fast fashion range in November 2005.

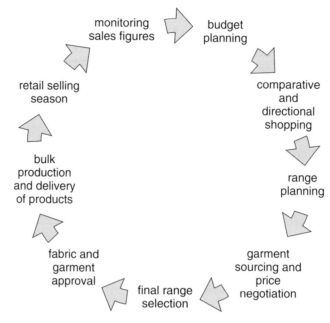

Fig 9.3 The buying cycle for own label fashion ranges. Adapted from Goworek (2001) p. 16

Range planning and selection

After planning the budget for the season and defining the number of styles required in a range in conjunction with the merchandiser working on the same product area (see Chapter 10) the own label buyer begins range planning. This involves compiling a commercially acceptable collection of garments within financial and design parameters, prior to production and delivery (Goworek, 2001). The range is aimed at a certain retailer, product area and season and must be suitable for the potential customer's lifestyle, co-ordinating with other products sold by the retailer at the same time. When buying a new season's range, the fashion buyer needs to plan the following:

- balance of different types of garment;
- specific product styles;
- fabrics, colours and prints;
- supply sources;
- selling prices;
- size ranges;
- order quantities.

The styling of the range is usually influenced by research during directional shopping trips by designers and buyers. Buyers should also familiarise themselves with the ranges sold by their competitors through comparative shopping, so that they can see the choice offered to their customers. Most fashion multiples select many of the designs from their suppliers but some retailers have their own in-house design teams, with whom buyers work closely (see Chapter 4). Several high street retailers collaborate with ready-to-wear designers to produce ranges which are exclusive to that store at much lower prices than the designer's main line, by manufacturing the garments more economically in large quantities (see Chapter 4). Department store Debenhams has led the field in this area by enlisting numerous prominent fashion designers such as Julien Macdonald for its 'Designers at Debenhams' collections. Buyers for these ranges liaise with the designers to develop garments which are suitable for the store's target customer whilst retaining the signature style of the designer. Swedish retailer H&M gained extensive publicity in 2005 for its collaborations with Karl Lagerfeld and Stella McCartney.

Buyers meet design and sales teams from suppliers to view design ideas for product ranges or to request samples of the retailer's own designs. Buyers can deal directly with overseas manufacturers, but are more likely to deal with an overseas sourcing office or a UK-based sales and design office with offshore manufacture. Buyers are responsible for selecting the countries and suppliers where the products in the range will be produced, usually from the retailer's existing supplier base. Despite the additional time and expense of delivering products from overseas, competitive production costs and a diminishing local manufacturing base have resulted in the vast majority of UK retailers sourcing fashion products globally. The press and pressure groups such as 'Labour behind the label' have raised various ethical issues about overseas garment sourcing in recent years and many retailers have now established ethical sourcing policies with which their suppliers must comply. Buyers and suppliers need to communicate effectively with each other as they liaise on a regular basis and have the same common aim to produce commercial styles which appeal to their customers. Buyers analyse the styles offered by the suppliers and review which products are most commercial in terms of design and price before selecting the range.

The final range selection is a significant meeting for the buyer, attended by senior managers such as buying and merchandising managers, when decisions are made about which styles are to be included in a range for a particular season. The buyer is responsible for presenting the range to colleagues, usually in the form of sample garments, and occasionally as drawings and fabric swatches. Samples are generally produced by suppliers but some fashion retailers have their own sample rooms. A range plan document is presented at the final range selection meeting including details of the styles which the buyer is proposing. The merchandiser supports the buyer in this meeting with financial information about the range. Some buyers may have pre-selection meetings beforehand with merchandisers, garment technologists and designers reviewing the range as a team. Senior managers need to approve the range which the buyer presents at the final range selection. Amendments to the range may be requested by the buying manager before it is signed off, with the aim of maximising the commerciality and profitability of the collection. Merchandisers can then place orders with the suppliers (see Chapter 10).

Fabric and garment approval

Most retailers have procedures to which the buyer and supplier must adhere to ensure suitable quality standards such as approving samples of fabrics and trims and fitting garment samples on models. These tasks are carried out in collaboration with garment technologists (see Chapter 7) and in some cases fabric technologists (see Chapter 6). Fashion buyers can spend much of their time communicating approvals and rejections to suppliers. Many fashion buyers are responsible for over 100 garment styles, so the progress and development of every item must be carefully documented, which is often the responsibility of the assistant buyer. Computer databases can be used to track progress and can be made accessible to buyers and merchandisers (and sometimes suppliers) through the company's intranet.

Monitoring sales figures

During the selling period of a garment range buyers and merchandisers have access to sales figures which they review at least once a week to identify sales patterns in the range (see Chapter 10). Buyers also visit stores to receive anecdotal feedback on sales from retail branch managers (see Chapter 11). The sales performance of a product can be assessed by volume of sales per style or financial turnover per style. Sales figures for the range can be compared to sales for the same period in the previous year, known as 'year-on-year' or against the sales forecast for the season by the merchandise team.

Fashion buying for mail order

Most large mail order companies employ teams of buyers and merchandisers to develop own label ranges in the same way as fashion retail chains. Like department stores, many mail order catalogues also stock branded merchandise, so they employ buyers for either own label or branded ranges. Because mail order products are sold through photographs rather than in stores, this can influence the mail order buyer's choice of products and the resulting sales figures. Photographic samples for mail order catalogues must be prepared well before the selling season, as publishing can take several weeks, so trends need to be predicted well in advance. Once product samples have been photographed for inclusion in the catalogue, the buyer has to ensure that products which look identical to the photograph are manufactured and delivered on time for the launch of the new season's range. Major companies in the UK mail order fashion market include GUS, Next and Grattan.

Fashion buying for the internet

Buyers for internet-based companies have similar responsibilities to retail buyers of either branded or own-label merchandise. In the UK, more products are now sold via the internet than from mail order catalogues. Companies such as yoox. com and net-a-porter sell designer merchandise trade through websites only and for this reason have become known as 'e-tailers' or 'pure players'. Some conventional bricks-and-mortar retailers sell the same products as their stores through websites, e.g. the Arcadia fashion multiples. Marks & Spencer are launching a selection of clothing and homeware through Amazon in 2006. Fashion chains which sell their ranges through stores, mail order and the internet are referred to as multi-channel retailers. Mail order companies are well-situated to sell online as the two methods are complementary, both being based on selling products from photographs, stocking merchandise in central locations and delivering merchandise by post. Selling through a website is a viable option for a small fashion business as start-up, staffing and distribution costs can be cheaper than operating a store.

CAREER ROUTES

Most large retailers employ trainee buyers who assist in the everyday running of the buying office, usually working on a specific range within a buyer's team. Another entry route is as a buyer's administration assistant (BAA) – a post which is obviously administrative and does not necessarily require a degree. However graduates could consider becoming BAAs with a view to applying for a trainee position. Most retailers value retail experience in their buyers and a fashion or textiles-related degree combined with a part-time job in a fashion retail outlet provides a useful background when applying to be a trainee buyer. Within a fashion multiple this role is likely to involve tracking the progress of products in the range.

Jane Shepherdson, brand director for Topshop, suggests the following strategy for those intending to start a career in fashion buying:

Try to get as much experience as possible in a buying office whilst still studying, either as a work placement, or over the holidays. This experience will probably get you an interview, as it shows that you know your way around and are keen, and it will enable you to be more effective when you start. The buyer's job is a combination of being creative and taking big risks with sometimes huge amounts of money involved, so unless you feel comfortable with both, it's not the job for you! And last, but not least, always trust your instincts.

After a year or more a trainee may become an assistant buyer which could involve responsibility for part of the buyer's product range and travelling abroad occasionally. It usually takes a minimum of four years working in buying to be promoted to buyer level. This is considered to be management or executive level in most retailers with the requisite salary and benefits. Buying managers (or controllers) are responsible for overseeing teams buying related products. The most senior job in this field is usually buying director, managing all buyers within the retailer, which can also include responsibility for the merchandising team. Generally, buying is one of the best-paid careers in fashion, especially in high street retailing, partly due to the rare blend of creative and commercial skills needed to do this job effectively. Many graduates from a wide range of fashion and textiles-related subjects are successful in finding jobs in fashion buying as design and technical knowledge are advantageous in this role. It is also possible to become a trainee fashion buyer with a degree in a different area, if the employer is convinced of the applicant's enthusiasm for fashion. Many fashion buyers later pursue careers in sales or set up their own businesses.

CASE STUDY

Buyer for a mass market fashion retailer

Career path

Helen Fahy has been men's knitwear buyer for River Island since 2004. After completing a BTEC National Diploma in Fashion Design she studied a BA (Hons) Fashion Marketing sandwich course. She graduated in 2001 and joined the buying team at River Island in the same year. As a student, Helen completed a work placement for swimwear and skiwear designer Sam de Teran as a production/design assistant, where she learned all aspects of how a small design company operates. She also worked for the former fashion retailer Richards as a sales supervisor and assistant manager during her degree course.

Responsibilities

Helen's team consists of an assistant buyer and a buyer's clerk. She reports directly to the buying controller responsible for men's knitwear, cottons, accessories and leathers. Helen describes her main responsibility as 'developing a well-balanced and profitable range' which involves:

- sourcing products from the right supplier in the right country for the right price;
- ensuring that developments are right for the customer and fit into the men's ranges and looks for the season;
- reacting to sales to ensure that the correct stock and repeats are available;
- being aware of fashion trends and what competitors are doing;
- managing and developing the men's knitwear buying team.

Based in River Island's head office in London, Helen's team is located next to the men's cottons team, so that they can work closely with each other and exchange ideas, as their products need to be displayed together in-store. A specialist men's knitwear designer who develops ideas for the range is a member of the in-house design team. Helen spends much of her time working with the merchandisers on her product area regarding critical path dates, margins, sales and quantities. Within the company, she also liaises with the QC department concerning fit samples and any quality issues. Helen is also responsible for supplying knitwear samples for the River Island website, brochure, press office and visual merchandising department. Helen has visited manufacturers in Hong Kong, China, Taiwan, Korea, Turkey and Italy as her knitwear range is produced in these countries. Helen takes part in relevant training and here she describes some of the courses provided for buyers by the company:

There are initial courses for new starters to ensure that they get the right training. There are also courses for different levels on a wide variety of things: negotiating, time management, coaching skills, personal development plans, etc. For new buyers or senior assistant buyers there is also a buying skills course.

Helen works towards a target customer profile for River Island when developing merchandise. Twice a year, she presents the new season range to her line managers and store managers, giving her the opportunity to receive feedback on customers' opinions of the men's knitwear collection. Helen says she also visits the stores 'to observe who the customer is first hand'.

Helen stresses the importance of teamwork and communication skills within her job:

The buying side works together with the designer to ensure we get a developed, well-balanced range. We work with the merchandiser to decide on how many options we will buy, in what quantities and how we are going to perform for the season. The rest of the buying team ensure that the orders I place are raised, suppliers have all the information they need and that the orders come in on time. If we didn't all work together we wouldn't get a range out into our stores. You have to be able to communicate well with other team members plus communicate with suppliers by e-mail, over the phone and face to face. For some suppliers English is not the first language so you have to be able to communicate what is required and to understand and respect the cultural differences.

Helen's performance at work is reviewed by her line manager and is measured against the job profile and priorities. She is also required to assess the performance of the staff she manages. Helen uses basic computer skills in her job as much of her work is carried out through e-mail, and she also uses Microsoft Word and Excel. She negotiates prices and works out cost prices and ratios for quantity, but the more complex calculations are handled by the merchandiser. Helen explains some of the other skills and abilities she needs as a buyer:

The basic technical skills I learned at university helped me to understand the make of a garment, but I didn't study knitwear, which is very different from wovens and jerseywear. I have learnt on the job and from discussing things with the suppliers. The ability to plan and organise is essential because you can be balancing four different ranges at once. You need to be able to plan your time so everything gets covered and nothing is missed. As a buyer it is important to be able to delegate jobs to your assistant otherwise there will not be enough time in a day for you to do everything. Management and coaching skills are important as your team need training and need to progress. Although not essential, a good memory is very useful, so you can remember all your styles across the season and last year.

Helen explains her favourite aspects of being a buyer:

The most exciting thing is when you see someone walking down the street wearing one of your garments. The development is exciting and seeing your ideas from a specification on a piece of paper to a sample, seeing how well it has worked. It's also great seeing sales and how styles performed: what works and what is a 'dog'. Travelling is great for getting to see places, though it can be very tiring as we work long days and it's hard work.

Career advice

When recruiting, Helen looks for self-motivated applicants, as buyers need to be able to work on their own as well as motivating the rest of the team. Buyers at River Island work closely with their designers so it is important that they can work on creative ideas as a team to develop the best possible range. When interviewing applicants Helen looks for people who are 'enthusiastic, passionate and have a flair for fashion'. She adds:

I think it's important to try and get as much work experience as possible to understand the industry and the job. It's useful to have an understanding of how a shop works and it gives you a great understanding of customers and how they shop. Buying is seen as a glamorous job but there is a lot of hard work and in the entry positions there is a lot of paperwork and administration, so be prepared to work hard but always be passionate and enthusiastic about what you do.

FURTHER READING

Books

Goworek, H. (2001) *Fashion Buying*. Blackwell Publishing, Oxford.

Magazines

Drapers
Lingerie Buyer

Websites

www.drapersonline.com
www.exhibitions.co.uk
www.lingerie-buyer.co.uk
www.moda-uk.co.uk
www.retailchoice.com

Fashion merchandising

Fig. 10.1 Liaision between fashion merchandisers and other roles

The role of the fashion merchandiser is to maximise a retailer's profitability by ensuring that the selected product range is delivered to stores in the right quantities at the right time. Co-ordination and liaison with internal departments and external suppliers are required to arrange for the product to be delivered to the retailer's warehouses and distributed to retail branches. The fashion merchandiser is usually responsible for:

- budget planning;
- attending range planning and selection meetings;
- placing orders with suppliers;
- reviewing the progress of the selected range;
- liaison with suppliers regarding production planning and deliveries;
- overseeing the allocation of stock to retail branches;
- evaluating product sales figures and supplier performance.

In some companies elements of the job described above are part of the buyer's role or may be performed jointly by the merchandiser and buyer.

Since fashion products are frequently referred to as merchandise, various roles within fashion retailing and manufacturing use the term merchandiser, such as visual merchandisers, who are responsible for the display of products within retail outlets (see Chapter 12). Some garment suppliers also employ staff known as merchandisers and this is similar to the retail merchandiser's role in that they also play a part in the delivery of fashion products to retailers (see Chapter 8). In the USA the term fashion merchandising is often used to encompass a broad range of activities relating to the marketing and retailing of fashion merchandise.

BUDGET PLANNING

Merchandisers plan the budgets for product areas, deciding the amount of money which will be available to buyers for a range for a particular season (known as 'open-to-buy'). Budgets are based on a combination of historical sales figures, mainly from the previous year, and forecasts for future sales. The budget is a projection of the amount of money the retailer will spend on buying merchandise from suppliers for the season and the sales turnover this is expected to generate. This could be influenced broadly by the financial performance and expansion plans of the retailer and general fashion forecasting. Apart from specific fashion trends, product types vary in popularity over a period of time, e.g. the recent move away from the fashion for trousers and increasing popularity of skirts and dresses in womenswear, so the amount of money committed to each product type may vary per season. In the era of 'fast fashion', an increased amount of many retailers' open-to-buy is retained for selecting products shortly before or during the season, to respond more quickly to fashion trends.

RANGE PLANNING AND SELECTION MEETINGS

Working within the agreed budget, merchandisers decide the number of lines to be included within the range for a product area. A merchandiser and buyer usually work together on the same range of products and may both carry out comparative shopping (see Chapter 9) to assess the product ranges offered by competing retailers. Merchandisers and buyers working on the same product area often have workspace located alongside each other within a team which can also comprise garment technologists and designers for the same range. Other retailers may prefer to situate the merchandising team separately, but there are obviously benefits to be gained from placing all those working on a product range together.

Merchandisers work closely with buyers to make recommendations for the range content, specifying product types and price ranges, which constitute the buyer's 'shopping list'. In some retailers merchandisers present 'range direction' meetings to give the buyers an initial brief before product development for a season commences, based on analysis of previous seasons' sales figures and supplier performance. Merchandisers attend pre-selection meetings with buyers to work with them on the numerical aspects of the range plan, such as profit margins, order quantities and size ranges. At final selection meetings the range is presented to senior managers by the buyer with the support of the merchandiser and the range plan is finalised.

PLACING ORDERS WITH SUPPLIERS

Purchase orders are generated by merchandisers for all of the products within the finalised range plan, mostly by using relevant computer software, which may have been tailored specifically to the retailer's requirements. A purchase order is a document containing all the relevant information about the product, which may also be known as a 'new line sheet'. The buyer provides the merchandiser with information on each style and the merchandiser adds quantities, size ratios and delivery dates. Purchase orders are sent by merchandisers to the appropriate suppliers, either electronically or as a hard copy and in effect this becomes a contract between the retailer and supplier containing all of the definitive details agreed on a particular style. Once orders have been placed, buyers and garment technologists can work with suppliers on product development to approve the fit, appearance and technical aspects of the garment in preparation for bulk production (see Chapter 7).

Order quantities and sales ranking

Own label retailers have styles made to order for them by suppliers and merchandisers estimate how much to order of each item. This is based on sales history of similar styles, trend predictions, advice from buyers and a certain amount of 'gut feeling'. To assist in this process, some retailers have 'sales ranking' meetings in which merchandise and buying teams assess the sales potential of all of the items within a range, producing a list of the products ranked by saleability. Merchandisers can place larger initial orders of the most popular styles or place the minimum order quantity whilst ensuring that they can buy more within the season should the product sell as successfully as predicted. At designer level and within branded ranges, styles are not made to order for retailers but are selected by buyers from ready-to-wear ranges, with the designer or brand taking the role of a wholesaler, and it is therefore possible for retailers to buy relatively small quantities.

Size ranges and ratios

Each retailer has its own sizing policy and the merchandiser or buyer decides which size range is suitable for each product, depending on the style. Since consumer demand for different sizes varies, merchandisers are normally responsible for deciding the proportion of an order to be allocated to each size, known as the 'size ratio' which is included in the order to the supplier. The example here shows the same size ratio expressed in figures and percentages. If 1000 pieces of this style were bought, the merchandiser would expect to receive 250 size 14 garments.

Garment size: 8 10 12 14 16 18 20
Buying ratio: 1   3   4   5   3   2   2
               5% 15% 20% 25% 15% 10% 10%

The best selling sizes are generally those in the middle of the range. Ordering products in the right size ratios can make a substantial impact on the retailer's turnover and profitability. Buyers usually take responsibility for deciding size ratios in small independent retailers, as they are unlikely to employ merchandisers.

Repeat orders

If a product sells well the merchandiser may consider placing a repeat order for this style with the supplier to meet customer demand. This needs to be organised as soon as the sales figures indicate high sales or there is a danger that the product will sell out. Merchandisers calculate the number of weeks 'cover' of a style, which means how long before the product is expected to sell out. A garment which sells 400 items in the first week for which 2000 pieces were ordered initially is liable to sell out four weeks later. For products from branded or designer ranges, the repeat order is placed with the original supplier if they have remaining stock of this style available. When a style has been designed in-house by a mass market retailer, repeat orders can be placed with the original supplier, but if that company cannot deliver in time, the buyer may develop a copy of the style with a supplier from a closer source for the repeat. This often means using a more expensive manufacturer, but as the sales are virtually guaranteed the merchandiser may be happy to accept a lower margin on this product.

Repeat orders are particularly important to mail order companies as customers will be disappointed if garments which they select from a catalogue are out of stock. Many fashion-led retailers may decide not to place repeat orders on styles as they prefer to offer each garment as a limited edition.

REVIEWING PROGRESS OF THE RANGE

Once purchase orders have been placed, merchandisers review the progress of each individual product in the range on a regular, often weekly, basis with buyers. This is to ensure that suppliers adhere to the critical dates for product development between ordering and delivery, so that merchandise will ultimately arrive in stores at the required time. Information on the submission and approval of fabric, trim and garment samples can be compiled on the retailer's intranet accessible to colleagues in merchandising, buying and garment technology departments, and in some cases suppliers.

LIAISON WITH SUPPLIERS

Merchandisers are in regular contact with their suppliers. Meetings between them may take place at the manufacturer's premises, giving experienced merchandisers the opportunity to travel overseas within their jobs. In some retailers merchandisers meet with sales and production planning staff from suppliers to anticipate the total amount of business the retailer may place with them in a given season. This is known as 'commitment' as the retailer is committed to using an agreed amount of garment production or fabric within a certain timeframe. When bulk production is completed, merchandisers can request the whole order to be delivered to the retail distribution centre (DC) in one drop or a schedule can be planned for a large order so that it can be manufactured and delivered in batches during the season, thereby using the retailer's storage space to its best effect. Merchandisers require constant updates from their suppliers on delivery dates and careful planning is required to achieve a balance between merchandise arriving on time and warehousing capacity.

ALLOCATING STOCK TO RETAIL BRANCHES

Merchandisers plan despatch from the DC, transport and arrival of the merchandise at stores throughout the country and overseas if necessary. The delivery of merchandise to stores to replace goods which have been sold is known as replenishment. The merchandiser aims to replenish stock at the rate at which is sold, either with repeat orders of existing items or new products. Too little stock makes the stores look sparse and limits the amount of products available for customers to buy. Too much stock causes a different problem: removing the excess products to make way for more profitable stock through promotional tactics or price reductions. Managing the distribution and delivery of stock during the selling period is often referred to as trading.

Merchandisers can gain feedback from store managers if problems arise with stock. As sales figures and selling space in each branch of a store chain vary, the merchandiser must offer an appropriate selection of products for the outlet. In most fashion multiples individual stores are graded, depending upon their size and location so that stores with the same grade receive the same variety of products, e.g. 'A' stores based in major cities usually stock the retailer's full range for the season. Spanish fashion chain Zara delegates some of the responsibility of allocating merchandise to store managers, who order quantities of styles from the retailer's range from head office, operating in a similar way to a buyer for an independent store.

The allocation of stock to stores is often part of an assistant merchandiser's job. Some retailers' merchandising teams may separate this function of the job from planning and analysis so it is carried out by allocators who may also be referred to as 'branch merchandisers', distributors, optimisers or stock controllers. Like fashion buyers, merchandisers can also be employed by mail order companies which retail products through catalogues, websites or TV channels (see Chapter 9).

EVALUATING PRODUCT SALES FIGURES AND SUPPLIER PERFORMANCE

Merchandisers monitor product sales on a regular basis and sales information is readily available through data from stores via electronic point of sale (EPOS) systems which scan barcodes at store checkouts. Sales figures are reviewed at least once a week by the merchandising team. At the launch of a new range sales are scrutinised daily to anticipate sales patterns for the rest of the season. The weekly sales, stock and intake plan (or WSSI, commonly known as 'Wizzy') is a document used by merchandisers to monitor sales and stock levels, usually in the form of a computer spreadsheet. When bestsellers (items achieving sales 'above plan') and 'dogs' (products selling 'below plan') are identified the merchandiser can decide on which action to take to rectify the situation.

Merchandisers and buyers may be offered bonuses within their employment contracts if sales achieve a specified level. Sales figures are analysed in total at the end of the trading period and the resulting analysis is shared with buying colleagues to make recommendations for future ranges. The attributes of bestselling merchandise can be updated for future seasons and the worst-selling products can provide valuable lessons about customers' preferences. Sales figures can also be analysed in further depth to review the performance of products by supplier. Suppliers with a consistently strong performance are likely to maintain or increase orders from the retailer and suppliers that perform poorly may be dropped by the retailer.

MERCHANDISERS WORKING FOR GARMENT SUPPLIERS

Merchandisers who work for garment suppliers arrange the transport and delivery of fashion products to retailers. Within a garment supplier, merchandisers ensure that products are despatched from the manufacturer to arrive at the retailer's DC at the specified time. The supplier's merchandising team is referred to as the logistics department within some companies. They liaise with their colleagues in sales and production planning to find out when deliveries are due and may also be involved in ordering the materials and trims from which products are manufactured. The supplier may have its own warehouse facilities to which stock is delivered from the factories or merchandise may be delivered directly to the retailer's DC, particularly if it has been manufactured overseas. As stated previously, the typical structure of a supplier is to have UK-based design and sales functions with offshore manufacture and this type of supplier may employ merchandisers in the UK or overseas.

CAREER ROUTES

It is usual for graduates to start a career in merchandising at trainee or assistant level. Certain companies employ allocators and this can be a starting position for someone wanting to progress into merchandising. After three years or more as a trainee it is possible to attain a merchandiser's position, with the resulting salary and benefits. In many retailers senior merchandisers or merchandise managers oversee merchandise teams. The most senior level in a retailer is usually merchandise director.

Merchandisers tend to earn similar salaries to buyers as they have an equal level of responsibility for product ranges within most retailers. It is feasible to progress into merchandising from a retail sales role as the knowledge of product, sales figures and customers gained by working in-store is extremely appropriate. As merchandising within a garment supplier is largely an administrative job it does not attract the salary or status of the retail merchandiser's position. Nick Atkinson, merchandiser for men's accessories at River Island advises:

> This is a fast-paced career and you need to be self-motivated and good at problem solving to succeed in it. I have 300 options to manage and it's very important to be able to communicate clearly and concisely as everyone needs to know what's going on with the product range.

As the merchandiser requires a combination of IT skills and commercial acumen, many fashion merchandisers have degrees in subjects such as business studies or computer studies. An interest in fashion products is also essential and it is possible for graduates of fashion-related subjects with a good numeracy or business knowledge to progress into fashion merchandising posts. There are currently two degree courses in the UK focusing on this area: London College of Fashion's BA (Hons) Fashion Management which offers a buying and merchandising pathway and University of Westminster's BA (Hons) Fashion Merchandise Management.

CASE STUDY

Senior merchandiser for a fashion multiple

Career path

Corri Homan-Berry is Senior Merchandiser for Footwear at New Look and has worked in merchandising for 11 years. She took A Levels in maths, business studies and theatre studies before studying a BTEC course in performing arts. She joined New Look straight from college as an office junior in 1993 then became a member of the merchandise team.

Role and responsibilities

Corri's main aim is to work with the footwear buyer to effectively plan and profitably trade the New Look footwear range. In order to achieve this aim her main responsibilities are:

- encouraging all members of the footwear team to reach their maximum potential;
- range planning;
- pre- and in-season stock and sales planning;
- taking trading decisions that maximise the performance of the range;
- maximising profit by ensuring that the flow of product through the supply chain is appropriately managed.

She is based at the company's head office in Weymouth, working with her team of merchandisers (see Fig. 10.2) alongside the optimisers who allocate products to specific stores. One of Corri's achievements at New Look was to establish the

Fig. 10.2 Corri Homan-Berry (left) participating in a planning meeting at New Look head office

larger size 'Inspire' collection. She has supported the growth of the footwear range which has increased by over 300 per cent over a five-year period, making it the second largest product area in the company.

Corri tries to spend at least one day per month in New Look branches and competing stores, as well as travelling to the Far East occasionally to visit suppliers. During October she is involved in trading the autumn/winter and Christmas range, buying products for the following year's spring launch and range planning for summer. At the same time she is working on the financial plan for the whole of the following year by forecasting sales volumes and expectations of sales turnover. She works in partnership with the buying team, logistics, retail, HR, IT and financial planning and also regards her suppliers as 'strategic partners'. She describes teamwork as critical, adding:

Buying, design and merchandising must work as a team to deliver a profitable and exciting range at the right time in the right stores in the right volumes. We also have to work with the rest of the business to ensure that our stores are prepared and have the information they need to display and sell the product. Our logistics and supply teams need us to work with them so they can bring the stock from the factories through to the shop floor. Cross-departmental teams are vital to the smooth delivery of our product.

As part of her job, Corri has been on IT training courses in Microsoft Word, Excel and Powerpoint as well as various personal development skills including negotiation and 360° feedback. She has also attended courses in range planning and essentials of merchandising, though she says most of her training is on the job, including the use of WSSI as a management tool to control stock levels and spending. When asked which aspects of merchandising she finds enjoyable and challenging she replies:

I love working with great people and bringing fantastic footwear to our wide customer base. Fashion moves fast and that makes my role challenging and exciting, never dull. The difficult parts of the job are staying calm under pressure, balancing exciting product with risk management, time management – we work to very tight deadlines – and ensuring that your team are highly motivated through the good times and bad.

Corri describes numeracy, planning and organisational skills as critical for a merchandiser. Other skills and knowledge she considers to be important are:

- communication;
- self-motivation;
- creative problem solving;
- computer skills;
- technical understanding of product manufacture;
- negotiation skills;
- influencing others.

She determines customers' requirements through sales data; feedback from buyers and designers; customer panels; the media; feedback from branch managers and talking directly to customers on store visits. Her performance is assessed through a combination of financial key performance indicators including sales and profit in her product area and demonstrating effective leadership. The success of the range is judged by its market share, staying within minimum and maximum stock parameters, reduction in markdown and profit margins.

Career advice

When employing merchandisers, Corri says she is looking for computer-literate, numerate interviewees who are:

- bright;
- enthusiastic;
- highly self-motivated;
- passionate about fashion with a commercial/retail background;
- eager to learn.

She advises those intending to work in merchandising:

> As well as the numerical, IT and technical skills to be a merchandiser, you have to be open-minded, prepared to work really hard and take on even the boring tasks with a smile.

FURTHER READING

Jackson, T. and Shaw, D. (2001) *Mastering Fashion Buying and Merchandising Management*. Macmillan, London.
Varley, R. (2001) *Retail Product Management: Buying and Merchandising*. Routledge, London.

Retail management

Fig. 11.1 Liaison between retail managers and other roles

Retail management is a term that can be used to describe a range of management level jobs within retailing, including buying, merchandising and visual merchandising. This chapter focuses specifically on the responsibilities involved in managing a fashion retail outlet. The retail manager's main aim is to maximise sales potential and profitability within a store by effectively combining management and commercial skills. The key responsibilities of fashion retail managers can be summarised as:

- managing sales staff and the store environment;
- motivating sales staff to achieve or exceed sales targets;
- recruiting and training suitable sales staff;
- reviewing and appraising the performance of sales staff;
- ensuring merchandise is presented and displayed appropriately;
- ensuring sales information and in-store promotions are used effectively;
- checking delivery and replenishment of stock on the shop floor;
- maintaining professional standards of customer service and responses to complaints;
- liaising with allocators or merchandisers regarding issues with stock;
- maintaining health and safety procedures for staff and customer welfare;
- overseeing store security.

To carry out these objectives fashion retail managers need to communicate effectively with staff and customers in the store and with colleagues at head office. The way in which retail managers operate is expected to reflect the company's brand values, which will be instilled during training.

MANAGING SALES STAFF

Retail managers are responsible for sales staff at various levels, most of whom are sales advisers, also known as assistants, associates or consultants, depending on the company. Sales advisers may be subordinate to senior advisers or supervisors who oversee a particular range of merchandise or area of the store, answering to the store manager. Sales staff may have particular responsibilities delegated to them in addition to retail sales, such as supervising the changing rooms. Retail managers participate in the recruitment process for sales positions within their stores in collaboration with the company's human resources (or personnel) department. After selecting, interviewing and appointing applicants retail managers need to plan training for new recruits in company policy and sales techniques or other skills if necessary. The team is likely to consist of full-time and part-time members of staff, as part-time jobs are obviously widely available in retail, often with increased staffing levels on a temporary basis leading up to Christmas. Retail managers organise staffing rotas and shifts, including delegating responsibility for the management of the store to deputies during their own absence. Having organised appropriate staff cover, store managers, their deputies or supervisors plan the team's workload from day to day, allocating specific tasks to the sales team including:

- staffing the sales counter;
- assisting customers in store;
- organising merchandise in the stock room;

- receiving deliveries of stock;
- distributing new merchandise within the store;
- recovering stock (see below);
- dealing with customer service queries.

In many stores, the branch manager is likely to participate in selling to customers on a regular basis or to cover for staff if necessary. Within the working day, the manager and senior sales staff need constantly to respond to the changing situation in the store depending on the flow of customers, reviewing the tasks assigned to sales advisers to achieve optimum service levels. Some of these tasks may need to be completed outside store opening hours and the retail manager has to plan for this, offering overtime hours if necessary. As the majority of fashion retailers open many of their stores seven days a week this can sometimes entail the manager and other team members working during the evening. Retail managers review the performance of sales staff through regular appraisals, identifying their strengths and weaknesses along with opportunities for training and promotion. Retailers must ensure that sales staff adhere to company policies and procedures and many stores have branch manuals available to the sales team to document these procedures and other relevant details pertaining to a specific outlet.

Retail managers have targets for the performance of the branch set by their line managers, which need to be communicated to sales staff. Productivity within the store can be assessed in numerous ways including:

- sales per employee;
- customers per day;
- sales per square metre.

Employing personal shoppers, or style advisers as they are sometimes known, is becoming popular with fashion retailers, offering customers the chance to book a free appointment to have an assortment of outfits selected to suit their lifestyles and personal tastes. Originally a luxury reserved for the rich and famous, various retailers have now adopted this service, realising that it is a productive way to gain multiple garment sales and win customer loyalty. John Lewis stores provide a personal shopping service, as do selected branches of House of Fraser and Topshop. If based in a single outlet, a visual merchandiser (VM) who organises the display of products in-store may answer to the store manager, though in many retailers VMs work across more than one store and are overseen by regional VM managers (see Chapter 12).

MANAGEMENT OF STOCK

The manager of a retail outlet is responsible for managing the journey of the company's products from their delivery into the branch, their layout in-store and subsequent sales to customers. Merchandise should be displayed in the windows and within the store to allow shoppers to buy the maximum amount with the minimum of input from sales staff through effective implementation of the retailer's VM policy, which is usually communicated via store layout plans issued to retail branches (see Chapter 12). Retail managers also need to oversee floor moves with sales and VM staff, primarily at the launch of new ranges, involving the reorganisation of fixtures and possible relocation of product types within the store. Store layout, sales information and in-store promotions should make shopping easy and enjoyable for customers. Effective price labelling is important for the convenience of customers but also to comply with legal requirements, e.g. sale prices must indicate the previous selling price in accordance with the Consumer Protection Act 1987.

'Look books' featuring drawings or photographs of a season's range are distributed to stores by many fashion retailers to enhance staff's product knowledge. This can encourage them to persuade customers to select co-ordinating outfits rather than purchasing single items. Stock should be constantly replenished (i.e. replaced) on the shop floor as quickly as possible during opening hours and at the end of each day (a process known as recovering) with merchandise from the stock room or new deliveries from suppliers or the retailer's distribution centre (see Chapter 10). It is not cost-effective for retail outlets to contain large stock rooms, as this prime retail space could be utilised more profitably for other purposes, so bulk quantities of merchandise are kept in central warehouses in economical out-of-town locations before being delivered to stores. Consequently retail outlets receive frequent deliveries of stock to replace product which has been sold, to minimise the space required to retain merchandise within the store.

Finance and security

The manager of a retail outlet is entrusted with a significant financial responsibility for sales transactions and stock within the store. Loss of stock through theft and damage is referred to as 'shrinkage'. The retail manager is responsible for opening up and locking the store in addition to storing cash and cheques from customer purchases and must carry out or delegate these duties to trustworthy colleagues on a daily basis.

CUSTOMER SERVICE

Retail managers aim to deliver good customer service in order to maximise sales. Each retailer has its own customer service policy which must take into account minimum legal statutory consumer rights. Retail managers are responsible for implementing the policy to ensure a consistent standard of service in branches nationwide. Some large retail outlets employ staff specialising in customer service, though it is essential for all sales staff to be briefed on the company's expected standards. Customer complaints often relate to unsatisfactory quality of products and lack of stock in the required size or style and the retail manager may be called on to pacify customers or rectify problems. Retailing experts Roger Cox and Paul Brittain (2004) offer the following advice in relation to customer complaints:

> *Even in the best run establishments there will be occasions when a customer is not completely satisfied and has cause to complain. It is here that the truly successful retailer will stand above the competition by converting a dissatisfied customer to a satisfied one who will return. With the high costs of marketing in today's highly competitive retail scene it is less expensive to resolve a current customer's problem than to win a new customer. (p.201)*

Fashion retailers' returns policies vary, but customers are legally within their rights to return faulty goods as products must be of 'merchantable quality' and 'fit for purpose' under the Sale of Goods Act 1979. In addition to these minimum rights many fashion retailers now offer customers the opportunity to return products for any reason within 28 days of purchase.

LIAISON WITH HEAD OFFICE

A retail manager's most regular contact with colleagues at head office is likely to be liaising with merchandisers, allocators or distributors regarding issues with stock replenishment or quality standards on a weekly or even daily basis (see Chapter 10).

Retail managers may also need to contact the distribution centre to chase up deliveries. Senior managers, buyers, merchandisers and designers often carry out store visits on a formal basis around the country to observe the product range *in situ* in different outlets and to gain valuable feedback about sales and customers from retail managers. Some retailers invite branch managers to presentations of new collections in advance of the selling season. This can be through a visual presentation or a fashion show presented by area managers or buyers, allowing the store managers the opportunity to preview the range and to suggest which styles are likely to appeal most to their customers.

TYPES OF RETAIL OUTLET

The main categories of fashion retail outlet in which retail managers operate are:

- fashion multiples;
- department stores;
- concessions;
- independent stores;
- outlet stores.

Most fashion multiples have well in excess of 100 stores, with centralised buying and merchandising functions. Fashion retailers can rent selling space within department stores as concessions in which they sell their own products and employ their own sales staff. Concessions can secure a wider presence for the retailer throughout the country more economically than setting up new branches. Outlet stores are often grouped together in out-of-town locations offering fashion merchandise at reduced prices. Most retailers have 'flagship stores' in London, or occasionally in other major cities, selling the company's complete range of merchandise and they may be used for promotional events, installing new shop fits and trialling new product concepts.

CAREER ROUTES

Fashion retail managers of individual outlets are not generally required to have a degree, though some companies seek graduates for senior positions in sales management. There are two specific courses available for those wishing to focus their studies in this area: BA(Hons) Fashion Retail Management at the University of Central England and BA (Hons) Retail Management with Fashion at the University of Central Lancashire. Entry level retail management jobs include departmental manager, floor manager or assistant/deputy manager. After gaining a year or more of experience in this type of post it may be possible to be promoted to branch manager level. Retail managers can earn significantly more than their sales staff and may also be given a clothing allowance and discount within the company's stores. A retail manager's salary for an individual store often depends on the size of the outlet, its location (salaries are usually higher in London), its target market and the number of staff.

The general manager of a retailer's flagship store or department store may earn the same salary as some area or regional managers. Area managers have usually managed a branch for several years and are responsible for a group of stores and their managers. Area managers' salaries in fashion chains can be equivalent to those of their colleagues in head office at buyer or merchandiser level and may partly consist of commission and bonuses based on the achievement of sales targets. They usually receive a company car, laptop and mobile phone as part of the benefits package to facilitate travelling between stores. The most senior job in sales with a retailer is to manage sales for the company at a national level, a role which may be referred to as retail operations manager or sales director.

One of the advantages of working as a branch manager for a fashion retailer is that it is possible to work in any region of the country, as opposed to being based in a central head office location. Retail experience can also provide entry to other management roles at head office such as buying or merchandising, particularly if this is combined with a relevant degree. Several recruitment agencies for fashion retail positions are featured in 'theretailbulletin.com' alongside news on retailing in the UK (see Chapter 18). Susannah Tomlinson, a recruitment consultant for Talisman Retail explains why it is a prerequisite in most fashion multiples for retail managers to have experience in fashion retailing:

Fashion stores will only consider people for retail management positions with fashion backgrounds as it is different to managing a food store, for example, which is much more task-orientated. Non-fashion retailers take on people with fashion experience, but not the other way round. It's not really important whether or not you're a graduate to be a fashion retail manager, but you need to be intelligent. You need to start making choices very early and get into the right retailer as soon as you can. I would recommend any student wanting this type of career to have a gap year with a fashion retailer, but it is very competitive with typically 30–50 candidates competing for two or three work placements. After graduating you can apply for a fast-track management trainee scheme as a floor manager. In department stores you can be promoted quite swiftly within a branch but they don't have many jobs for area managers. Very few area managers' positions are actually advertised so the best thing to do is to prove yourself within the business by moving to managing large turnover stores within a fashion multiple as soon as you can, to give you a springboard into area management.

CASE STUDY

Retail sales manager

Career path

Sue Stones has been womenswear sales manager at Harvey Nichols' Edinburgh branch for three years. She studied fashion design then worked for Jaeger in product development in their London studio. On moving to Edinburgh she joined an independent department store, Jenners, where she worked on the shop floor for a year prior to joining their management training scheme. She was then promoted to assistant buyer for hosiery and accessories before becoming buyer for designer womenswear. After nine years at Jenners she moved to Harvey Nichols in 2002 in her current role to set up and open the new store (see Fig. 11.2).

Fig. 11.2 Harvey Nichols' Edinburgh store
Courtesy of Harvey Nichols

Role and responsibilities

Sue is responsible for the sales and profits of the womenswear floors, including personal shopping, in the Edinburgh store. She is in charge of over 70 people in full-time and part-time sales positions (see Fig. 11.3) and describes her main responsibilities as:

- managing staff;
- sales and customer service;
- research and development;
- acting as a member of the senior management team;
- concession liaison.

Sue's aims are to ensure the best levels of customer service and highest sales capacity. She arranges staff training and handles any disciplinary action that is required with the support of the HR team. She has studied training courses in management skills and team development. She is involved in setting sales targets, monitoring results and giving feedback to the buying and merchandising team to maximise profit. She explains some of the regular tasks she carries out:

I review the sales and costs every day and every week and meet with the store manager on a monthly basis to review performance against budgets. Any customer service issues are also referred to me to resolve and it is important that I spend time with the sales teams to ensure they have the required product knowledge and are aware of the importance of maintaining service standards. As Womenswear Sales Manager it is important that regular discussions take place with my other sales colleagues in menswear and accessories. This way the store runs as a whole rather than three entities and we ensure fairness and uniformity for staff and customers throughout. As senior managers we are

Fig. 11.3 Structure of the womenswear sales department at Harvey Nichols' Edinburgh store

expected to act as duty manager for the store in the absence of the general manager should events require it.

Sue has more opportunity to be involved in research and to influence the buyers than sales managers in many retailers would have:

I am constantly researching the fashion industry to build my knowledge of new brands and designers. I encourage feedback from staff and customers to ensure that we have both the correct brand range and the right balance of product from each designer. The buyers and merchandisers depend on us to let them know what our customers' require- ments are. They are highly receptive to the informal feedback we give them daily and through formal meetings before the buying season commences. The input we have is essential to ensure that we have the right stock for the customers when they want to buy it.

Sue is the main point of contact for concession staff and area managers and is responsible for ensuring that their sales targets are met and that staffing levels and stock levels are maintained. She also manages visual merchandising within her department. When asked to describe an average day at work Sue says:

There is no typical day and that is what appeals to me most about my job. I often make plans about what I would like to achieve for the day but these are often disrupted. I start by looking at the figures for the week against what we should achieve, analyse why they are better or worse than forecast and act on any decisions made, for example speaking to buyers about stock, remerchandising the shopfloor or motivating the sales teams. I then check that there are no outstanding issues to be dealt with on the sales floors and update the general manager on the sales position and if we are likely to achieve target.

Sometimes I spend all day talking to staff and customers about fashion, designers, celebrities, clothes, shoes and at other times I spend all day poring over columns of sales and stock figures. Working with beautiful things and like-minded people in a high fashion environment is ideal for me as part of a selling team. I still enjoy the buzz from meeting sales targets and satisfying customers' expectations. The most difficult aspects are also people-related: dealing with unhappy customers or staff can be the most chal- lenging aspect.

Sue rates teamwork as 'imperative for a retail store' and says 'it is constant and appropriate to all levels of the business, we would not survive without it'. The other skills and qualities she considers to be important within her role are:

- sense of humour;
- love of fashion;
- self-motivation;
- confidence;
- sociability;
- diplomacy;
- experience;
- flexibility.

Career advice

Sue describes the main qualities the company looks for when employing retail managers:

> *We look for people who are enthusiastic, committed and have integrity. We want them to love selling and enjoy meeting people. They need to have good people skills and be able to motivate and challenge others in their team to achieve their potential.*

Her advice to those considering a career in fashion retail is:

> *Don't go into retail for the money. It's not about how much you're paid – it's about enjoying your job. If you like people you'll love retail.*

FURTHER READING

Books

Cox, R. and Brittain, P. (2004) *Retailing – an Introduction*. Pearson Education, London.
Varley, R. and Rafiq, M. (2004) *Principles of Retail Management*. Palgrave Macmillan, London.

Magazines/journals

Drapers
In-store
International Journal of Retail and Distribution Management
Retail Week

Websites

www.instoremagazine.co.uk
www.retailchoice.com
www.retail-week.com
www.theretailbulletin.com

Visual merchandising

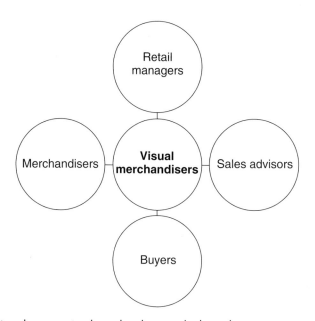

Fig. 12.1 Liaison between visual merchandisers and other roles

Visual merchandising (VM) is often described as 'the silent salesperson' and is defined by Pegler (1998) as 'displaying merchandise with the aim of maximising the volume of product sales'. VM is responsible for enticing as many target customers as possible into the store through effective window displays and encouraging them to buy through the skilful layout of products in store. VMs need a natural flair for composition and layout, with an appreciation of the store's target customers and what appeals to them. Awareness of the company's brand image is essential, combined with knowledge of products and display techniques. In a given season the main garment trends and colour stories will be similar throughout the high street and several stores within one location may sell some identical branded products at the same prices. VM methods can help to differentiate a retailer's brand image and product range from those of its competitors. A wide variety of equipment and techniques are available to the VM with which to implement their creative skills, including permanent and moveable fixtures and fittings such as mannequins, shelves, racks and stands. The main creative elements of displaying products which can be utilised within VM include:

- colour;
- texture;
- settings, furniture and props;
- composition.

WINDOW DISPLAY

Window display is the most obvious aspect of the VM's craft and its aim is to lure 'window shopping' customers into the store. The ways in which products are displayed in the window give the retailer a brand image which influences customers' current and future purchases. The VM should aim to portray an image through the window display which is aspirational yet achievable for the target customer. The traditional term for this skill is 'window dressing' and it is an aspect of VM which has become highly regarded as a method of contributing towards a fashion retailer's profitability. VMs select appropriate, eyecatching merchandise for the window display though it is acknowledged that customers often buy more basic products once they enter the store. The emphasis may be on a single outfit or a collection of similar or varied products (see Fig. 12.2). Styles which are striking, typify the season's key trends or look their best on the figure are chosen for the window. Some garments may not have 'hanger appeal' (i.e. their shapes do not look particularly attractive on a hanger), but they may be shown to their best advantage when worn by a mannequin.

Fig. 12.2 Vivienne Westwood window display in Selfridges, London, 2005
Courtesy of Selfridges

Enclosed and open-backed windows

Store windows may have enclosed displays or open backs, giving a tempting glimpse inside as the customer passes by, or they may be partially screened-off, e.g. with opaque or transparent panels. The VM ensures that the partial view into the store is pleasing to the customer and that from inside, the back view of the window display looks tidy. An enclosed window has the advantage that the back view of products is concealed from people in the store, allowing the opportunity for pins and bulldog clips to be used at the back of the mannequins to drape and fit the garments. Parts of the store window can be masked off to focus on small visible sections. This economical technique has been used by department store Debenhams and it can attract customers to look more closely because it varies from their usual expectations.

Seasonal events

Store windows are changed frequently to maintain customers' attention. This can be as often as once a week, though each retailer has its own policy. Window displays are often changed in preparation for seasonal events, such as Valentine's Day and the January sales. VMs compose seasonal sales promotions which need to be eyecatching without putting too much emphasis on specific products.

Signage

Signage on a window can be an effective method for retailers to notify customers of specific events such as new product launches without needing to incur the costs of press advertising. The windows within the numerous branches of fashion chains can be used as free advertising space for the company to disperse information to the vast numbers of customers passing by. In 2001, Marks & Spencer successfully publicised the launch of the Per Una collection by regularly updating signs with a countdown of the days to its arrival in the windows of relevant branches. The anticipation created by this promotion may have contributed to the initial sales targets for Per Una being exceeded.

IN-STORE DISPLAY

VMs display products in the store to enable customers to spend as much as possible requiring the minimum of help from staff. This can save the store resources as it allows staff to concentrate on other elements of their jobs, whilst giving customers the freedom to shop without being interrupted by sales advisers. Within reason, all display opportunities in the store should be exploited, if sufficient budget is available, so that there are no empty spaces unless the aim is to intentionally create a minimal look.

Fashion multiples buy modular display systems which can be adjusted to the different sizes and proportions of their various branches. The VM decides how to

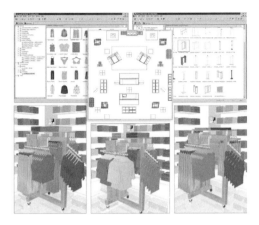

Fig. 12.3 Lectra 3D Visual Merchant – Visual Merchandising and Assortment Planning software
Courtesy of Lectra

adapt the display of the retailer's stock to each outlet. The VM and branch manager may make joint decisions on the location of the mannequins and fixtures within a particular outlet. Store designers select or develop the fixtures and VMs are responsible for ensuring that they are used as effectively as possible to encourage customers to make impulse purchases.

Standard window displays and in-store layouts are developed by VM managers for fashion multiples. Photographs are taken of the finalised ideas to be compiled into 'look books' to distribute to the company's branches to implement a consistent appearance throughout the chain of stores. Since most large fashion retailers open seven days a week it can be difficult to find space to test layouts without restricting customers from shopping in one of the branches. This problem can be overcome by having 'mock shops' at the retailer's head office so that a central VM team have a replica store permanently available to which customers have no access. 'Mock shops' are very expensive in terms of the space they consume and computer programs provide a more cost-effective option. Software can be used by VMs to design the layout of merchandise and test alternative ideas without taking up the space and time to move the merchandise around physically, with the added benefit that the images can easily be printed out for distribution to the store's branches (see Fig. 12.3).

Mannequins

Mannequins are most frequently used in window displays but may also be used within the shop, particularly in larger outlets such as department stores, where they can be used to communicate visually to the customer the location of different product ranges, such as young, branded fashion or lingerie. Many styles of mannequin are available, from solid dummies with a realistic appearance to padded, doll-like childrenswear figures. Mannequins usually have a lifespan of

Fig. 12.4 Ira mannequins from Adel Rootstein
Courtesy of Adel Rootstein

around three years in terms of fashionability, depending on the market sector, so they need to be replaced regularly to maintain a fashion retailer's contemporary image. Headless mannequins are more classic, as they have no features, and can be more economical, as they require updating less often, can fit into a smaller space, and don't detract from the clothes. However, they give the VM less opportunity to create and sell a complete fashion image.

Sculpted sections of the body, such as the torso, bust or legs, known as 'forms' are often used in-store for a 3D display of specific categories such as lingerie, swimwear or trousers. Specialist companies sell mannequins and forms (see Fig. 12.4) and they are also featured in trade fairs and websites. Instead of using mannequins, VMs can opt to show products on hangers, draped on chairs or suspended by wire. To dress a mannequin or form, the VM irons the garment, pins excess fabric towards the back and finishes it with a handheld steamer.

Racks

The VM department selects certain items to be displayed front-facing in store. As in the window display, the products promoted within the store are changed at regular intervals to vary the look and to encourage customers to notice items which they missed on a previous visit. This can involve simply changing the products on racks in their existing locations, moving groups of products to different parts of the store or relocating the racks within the shop. In virtually every fashion store a large percentage of merchandise is displayed on racks, giving customers a side view of garments. Stocking clothing on racks is economical in its use of space, which is beneficial to retailers in all areas of the market.

Gondolas, stands and cases

Gondolas are long fixtures which are often used on the shop floor. They may have storage space such as drawers with display shelves above and are suitable for displaying various product types together as different sizes of storage incorporated into the same fixture. Stands may be placed on gondolas or sales counters and can be used to display small items such as jewellery and scarves. Glass cases can be used individually or incorporated into the sales counter and are used to present expensive products such as watches, as they offer better security than other shop fixtures.

Shelves

Shelves are ideal for displaying small items such as shoes. Footwear retailers Qube and Brantano rely extensively on shelving, offering the full range of sizes directly to the customer without requiring the assistance of sales staff. More established footwear stores such as Dolcis and Clarks currently prefer to use the more traditional method of displaying one or two shoes in popular sizes necessitating the intervention of sales advisers to allow customers to make a purchase.

Shelves are frequently used to display basic merchandise which can be folded easily such as jeans, plain-coloured sweatshirts and T-shirts where customer buying decisions are likely to be made primarily on colour. This is an economical way to display in terms of space as the maximum amount of merchandise can be fitted into a relatively small space, but it can be time-consuming for shop staff to maintain a tidy appearance. The shape of a garment can be shown by displaying a front-facing item in one of the colourways or clear black and white technical drawings alongside the shelves.

CAREER ROUTES

It is not vital to be a graduate to work in VM, since many people have progressed into it from being sales advisers, but a fashion or textiles qualification could be advantageous when combined with retail experience. Fashion marketing, management or promotion degrees often contain VM within the curriculum and the London College of Fashion offers short courses in this subject. When working for a small retailer VM may be combined with a sales role. In general, VMs earn less than many other fashion and textiles-related jobs though it is possible to be well-paid for freelance VM work, supplying a service to various retail customers (see Chapter 17). Large retailers usually have national and regional VM managers who can earn competitive salaries, responsible for developing store display and layouts and managing in-store VMs. VM consultants work independently, providing advice to retailers on VM strategy and are generally the most highly-paid in this field. Jenny Swartout, a consultant with specialist retail training and consultancy First Friday advises:

A VM career can take many paths. It could take you along a creative route – implementing windows and in store displays to designing window schemes and training store staff in display techniques, or a more strategic role in planning and merchandising stores to maximise sales. VMs need creative flair, but it is important to remember that visual merchandising is not just about using windows and displays to show products at their best. It is also about increasing sales through the appropriate use of space, fixturing and product – for this an understanding of retail, marketing and customer behaviour is crucial. Experience of working in a retail environment can be helpful – and retailers often recruit internally from store level and train visual merchandisers inhouse. Finally, use what's around you to train yourself. Every time you shop think how the retailers entice customers into their stores and how they encourage customers to shop.

CASE STUDIES

Head of VM for a department store

Career path

Erin Thompson has recently been appointed head of VM and 3D for Selfridges. After studying an art foundation course and BA(Hons) Fashion and Textiles, she worked at Mulberry Company for 12 years, where she became creative services manager. She was responsible for Mulberry wholesale and retail worldwide and had a very varied role: from designing exhibition stands, showroom interiors, window displays and in-store presentation to planning and setting up stores throughout Europe and the Far East. Erin has worked at Selfridges for four years, initially as part of a team focusing on opening new stores, and was involved in developing the Birmingham store for 18 months before it opened.

Role and responsibilities

Erin lists her main responsibilities as:

- window and in-store presentation across all four Selfridges stores (London, Birmingham and two Manchester branches);
- forward planning for future events and promotions;
- running and maintaining the retail environment.

Forward planning starts with a creative brief from Selfridges' creative director Alannah Weston, then Erin works with her team to translate this into a 3D form in the window displays and in-store. Erin explains how she works with a variety of people to create VM and display concepts:

Internally we need to work closely across all the functions of the business; from Buying and Merchandising, Retail Operations and Marketing to Design and Development. Then there are our suppliers, people we rely on completely to enable us to deliver each project and promotion. The everyday ongoing running of the stores should not be underestimated. It's a fast moving business, we need to react to trade and turn things around quickly as well as maintain and recover the store each day. Sometimes we also work with external consultants who may be brought in from other fields like Michael Howells, a production designer from the world of film and advertising who worked on Orlando and the Versace advertising that featured Madonna for Spring/Summer 2005. He is inspirational and has worked with me and my team developing our Christmas 2005 scheme. For specific projects or events we try to work with celebrity designers, artists and photographers, etc. The criteria for choosing these people can vary per theme or event. We commissioned David La Chapelle to design our Vegas Supernova windows in 2005, as his work is very Vegas and his set designs were part of our original inspiration for the whole promotion.

Erin's team includes a 3D manager who is responsible for window displays across all four stores (see Fig. 12.5). The 3D team covers creative, production and styling aspects and consists of 10 people. The fashion VM manager and her team cover creative, styling and merchandising for three-and-a-half floors of the Oxford Street store. The lifestyle VM manager and his team are responsible for the food-hall, all catering outlets and home products in the Oxford Street store. The project manager works on Christmas virtually all year and is responsible for other smaller projects including sourcing or designing new fixturing and specialist lighting for VM sites and managing the signage studio. The regional VM Manager co-ordinates and supports the three regional stores. Erin has to work within the limitations of time, budget, manpower, commerciality and viability, although she says:

On the whole we are very lucky, we have some great product and fantastic spaces to work with. There are set lead times for things like mannequin production and prop manufacture, we are forever trying to beat the clock. For example, we started working on our Christmas theme in March this year and actually that was late, so next year we aim to start even earlier.

Erin visits Selfridges' regional stores regularly. She also travels abroad to find inspiration for the store's major promotions with recent trips to Brazil and Las Vegas. She has been to China to source Christmas props and decorations and aims to visit New York once a year. She often travels to fashion trade fairs with the

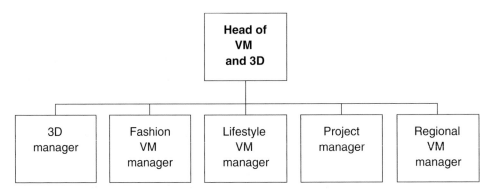

Fig. 12.5 Management structure of the VM and 3D department at Selfridges

buying team as well as doing comparative shopping. Erin clearly enjoys her job but also faces challenges within her management role:

I love working with my team and brainstorming ideas for future seasons in addition to working with external designers and architects, when we are redesigning areas of the stores. But the main kick is starting with an idea, being instrumental in developing that idea into life and then making it happen. There are lots of tough bits of the job and I have to be able to work closely with my team yet maintain enough distance to effectively manage them. I have to deal with positive and negative feedback and so does every member of the team. In our world, there are lots of opinions and deciding which ones to listen to can be difficult. We can work on initial ideas and themes that might never be developed further. It's important to take any emotion out of the equation and not take anything too personally. Teamwork and communication are fundamental to everything we do and they need to be consistently and constantly happening. The London store is the size of an ocean liner parked on Oxford Street, with up to 4000 people working in the building, and nothing happens without good teamwork.

Career advice

Erin describes VM as 'a real mix between the creative and the practical'. When interviewing applicants for jobs in her team she looks for 'team players' with a blend of the following skills and abilities, depending on the specific role she is recruiting for:

* communication skills;
* self-motivation;
* creativity;
* computer skills;
* technical skills;
* the ability to manage a budget;
* planning and organisational skills;
* common sense.

Erin points out some of the main things she feels would be useful for someone embarking on a career in VM to know:

At the start VM is all hands-on and it's hard graft. People don't realise how physically demanding it can be: you are up and down ladders, you can walk miles in one day around the store and you are constantly carrying and moving heavy props. As you progress, the job changes and computer skills become more important. We use Photoshop for window visuals, Quark for graphics and Vector Works for layouts, plans and fixture drawings. Nowadays, VM has a lot of different aspects to it: my team consists of stylists; visualisers; experienced managers; great creative ideas people and practical people. As a student I didn't know VM existed, I fell into it after leaving college and I loved it. This career can exceed your wildest expectations.

Visual merchandiser for a branded fashion retailer

Career path

Leanne Worsley has been a VM for French Connection in Manchester since 2003. She started working in fashion retail part-time at the age of 16 whilst studying for a BTEC National Diploma in Interior Design, and worked for several retail chains before joining French Connection in 2000 as a store manager.

Responsibilities

Leanne works on the basis of two seasons per year: August to December for autumn/winter merchandise and February to July for spring/summer, and both seasons are split into four packages, with January being devoted to sales. When she was a store manager for a smaller branch of French Connection, which operated as a franchise, Leanne was also involved in VM as she did not have a full-time member of staff to do this. As a result, she gained the necessary experience to move into a permanent VM position in a much larger outlet owned directly by French Connection. Leanne defines her daily responsibilities in the store as:

- ensuring new items are displayed in a commercial way, making them easy for the customer to make a purchase;
- checking sales figures to identify bestsellers and boost sales;
- replacing items which sell out (which may involve moving fixtures depending on the item);
- checking dates for new deliveries of products;
- training all staff in the company's VM standards;
- checking staff's standards of VM;
- managing major fixture moves.

The company has a display team which takes overall control of the windows and mannequins, and a marketing team responsible for signage and graphics within their outlets. As well as being based in store, Leanne is part of a team of ten VMs who work for the brand across the UK. The team meet in the London flagship store once a month to plan the display of new ranges of merchandise and the team have to work through the night to give them enough time to decide jointly on the colour stories and layout of the stock. The results are then photographed and sent to all French Connection outlets in the UK for them to copy in order to maintain a consistent brand image. Leanne's line manager oversees the implementation of VM throughout the country and each area VM is responsible for a cluster of seven to eight small stores (see Fig. 12.6). French Connection also have VMs operating in Ireland, Europe, Asia, Australia and the USA.

Leanne explains some of the work she carries out with colleagues in store and at head office:

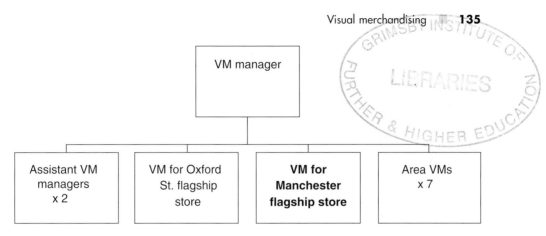

Fig. 12.6   The structure of French Connection's visual merchandising team in the UK

We do fixture moves every so often to create a change of layout and moveability around the store. I occasionally help to do floor moves at near-by stores. We can put ideas about layout to the VM manager and we can try them out on the overnights. Although gruelling, the overnight is a good chance for the whole team to get together and get some ideas into practice. It's also nice to see the final look in your store. The VMs also get together for range reviews which give us an opportunity to see the whole season's stock before it is launched.

It is important to get involved with retail management as they are the ones selling the items and they have a good idea of what sells best. Teamwork is extremely important. You also need to work as a team with people in your outlet if you are an in-store VM working to boost target sales and to keep the shop looking great. I also keep in regular contact with the buying and merchandising team at head office by email and phone, to find out what's going on if any problems with stock occur, such as best-sellers or faulty products.

Career advice

Leanne rates the following skills as the most important for VMs:

- communication;
- planning and organisation;
- self-motivation;
- creativity.

When employing VMs Leanne looks for people who are very enthusiastic about the job, as they often need to work long hours and travel. She adds:

Patience is needed when training staff. Also it can take a while to get to grips with VM as whole so you need a lot of determination. Each store has a slightly different layout and size, so you have to plan carefully to fit all of the stock in. VMs have to communicate about what does and doesn't work and to explain their ideas. You need to have a huge interest in fashion to be able to put styles together and be really creative.

FURTHER READING

Books

Bell, J. A. (2006) *Silent Selling: best practices and effective strategies in visual merchandising.* Fairchild, New York.

Diamond, J. and Diamond, E. (1999) *Contemporary Visual Merchandising.* Prentice-Hall, New Jersey.

Pegler, M.J. (1998) *Visual Merchandising and Display.* Fourth edition. Fairchild Publications, New York.

Magazines

Drapers
In-Store
Visual Merchandising and Store Design (VM + SD)

Websites

www.fashionwindows.com
www.rootstein.com
www.visualstore.com

Fashion PR

By Helen Kenny

Fig. 13.1 Liaison between fashion PRs and other roles

Fashion PR (public relations) is the business of creating, promoting and maintaining a good public image for and manipulating the public's perception of a product or brand. The key word in this definition is *image*. The fashion PR creates this image by mediating between his or her client – who may be a brand manager, designer or retailer – and the press. It is the responsibility of the PR to ensure that the client receives press that is beneficial. The world of fashion PR spans the whole of the fashion spectrum, from Chanel couture to Florence + Fred at Tesco. The glamour of the brands may vary greatly but the basic principles behind PR remain the same regardless of the identity of the client. No two PRs' jobs are exactly the same and on a day-to-day level the PR's role and responsibilities may vary greatly.

However, there are various tasks and duties which most PRs share in common: broadly speaking, all PRs deal with client management and press liaison. Fashion PR is concerned with building and sustaining relationships with key members of the press. PR is a very social career and involves interaction with a wide variety of fashion people. PRs have to remember their opinions and ego come second to the clients and journalists and their hours are dictated to by the client's needs, not by a fixed contract.

CLIENT MANAGEMENT

Clients, whether they are designers or brand managers, are the most important people the PR deals with. The PR has to ensure that the client's demands, if realistically possible, become reality. These demands will centre around the kind of PR the client sees as appropriate. The requests clients make may sometimes be very demanding but as the clients pay the PR company, it is essential they are happy. The relationship between the PR and client is crucial and is maintained by the PR's ability to be diplomatic and, most importantly, achieve results.

One way PRs can display proof of their achievements is by using cuttings books of various press cuttings featuring the client's products, which the PR takes credit for generating. Cuttings books are arranged according to the type of press coverage: one book may house regional material, another may contain tabloid press and a third could include coverage from glossy magazines. Cuttings books are normally updated on a weekly basis by a junior PR. The process involves trawling through publications and looking for successfully secured press. This process is quite often followed by a weekly meeting in which PRs discuss the strengths and weaknesses behind their current press coverage and their action plan for moving forward. To attract new clients PRs put together a pitch. This involves making the PR and the company's connections obvious and explaining how these contacts can be used to secure more successful press coverage for the potential client.

PRESS LIAISON

Press releases offer a solid point of contact between the PR and fashion journalist. Fashion journalists receive a vast number of press releases from all the various fashion PRs. It is the PR's job to write press releases so that they capture the journalist's attention. The most successful press releases are entertaining whilst being succinct, to the point and conveying all the necessary information. Although press releases offer a tangible and solid point of contact between the PR and the journalist a large proportion of the fashion PR's time is spent building relationships with fashion journalists and stylists. At the PR week conference 'PR and the Media' in March 2005 Dylan Jones, Editor of *GQ*, stated:

> *In the last issue of GQ, of 155 editorial pages, over half were generated by PR. GQ is full of PR-generated material and this usually stems from personal relationships.*

This quote illustrates the enormous influence that PRs wield over the content of fashion magazines. The quote also demonstrates the extreme importance of personal relationships in PR. Fashion journalists and stylists are notoriously busy and difficult to get hold of, especially if they are important – and these are exactly the ones PRs want to build relationships with. One way of securing busy journalists' attention is to offer them a very expensive free lunch. This is one of the major perks of being a PR. The luckiest fashion PRs spend a considerable amount of their work time having glamorous meetings over afternoon tea or lunch. This is not such a frivolous working task as it sounds. Once a fashion PR has secured a meeting with a key journalist the work does not stop there: the meeting will be used to try to gain imminent future press coverage or consolidate a fragile working relationship. Over time the relationship between the journalist/stylist and PR may become more relaxed, yet the PR can never forget that essentially they are responsible both for maintaining a working relationship with the important member of press and getting their clients promoted.

THE PRESS EVENT

Press events are held at key promotional times and offer yet another valuable point of contact between the journalist and PR. There are two main occasions that may call for a press event to be held: when a new product is added to a brand, or when the seasons are changing over. Press events vary in their significance and level of theatricality. Some PRs may simply invite journalists into their showrooms to give them an opportunity to view their new collection, whilst others may throw a huge party with celebrity guests after their main fashion show. Whichever option is chosen for the press event it will mean a lot of work and organisation for the PR. PRs are responsible for ensuring that the correct journalists see the product or collection that they are promoting. The process begins with the PR writing a press release; this will outline in a persuasive manner the appeal and relevance of the product or collection. This may be sent along with a more imposing and visually appealing invitation. The PRs involved in the organisation of the press event are responsible for chasing up the invitation and collecting RSVPs. For the more extravagant press events the management begins to get complicated; in these cases a location, catering, entertainment or even travel arrangements may become part of the organisation and responsibilities.

PR AGENCIES AND IN-HOUSE PRs

A PR agency normally deals with more than one client. There are advantages and disadvantages to working within an agency. An agency's variety of clients means that the PR will get an experience of working with different names and brands. On the downside, agencies also have the reputation for being hotbeds of office politics and subtle hierarchy. This situation can arise in agencies as there is normally a large team of PRs and many of them are chasing the same glamorous accounts and promotions. However, this problem can be easily avoided; simply by asking around the industry it is possible to gauge an agency's reputation. In-house PR refers to the retailer, brand or designer exclusively employing PRs as part of the company infrastructure. This situation means there is normally a much smaller team employed and a much clearer hierarchy.

WHAT MAKES A GOOD FASHION PR?

The role of the fashion PR is primarily concerned with communication. PRs spend every day discussing and promoting their clients. This means fashion PRs have to have excellent verbal and written communication skills. All fashion PRs need to possess an obsessive knowledge of and passion for the fashion industry. The successful fashion PR will know key and relevant journalists, the trends of the season, publication deadlines, and have impeccable knowledge of the brands and products they promote. The best fashion PRs have extreme social dexterity and charm and are able to show a very convincing enthusiasm for a brand, client or journalist that is not necessarily to their taste. The fashion PR also needs to be very diplomatic and discreet, as they are privy to and often the first to hear all the gossip and rumours of hiring and firing. Journalists and stylists frequently use their meetings with PRs to offload their anxieties and frustrations about office politics.

A good PR has an ability to deal with very demanding and sometimes unreasonable clients and members of the press, whilst keeping calm under duress. The working relationship a PR has with a client is not dictated by predictable office hours – if there is a press event or catwalk show to be organised PRs often find themselves working very unsociable hours. In addition, journalists are not usually patient people. A successful PR company deals with impatient members of the press asking the impossible on a daily basis. This could range from an overambitious journalist demanding show tickets to which they are not entitled, to a fashion assistant requesting that a clothing sample arrives in the next hour.

CAREER ROUTES

It is not essential to have a relevant degree to work in fashion PR as an enthusiasm for fashion and interpersonal skills are considered to be more important. However, graduates of fashion or textiles-related courses often pursue careers in PR. A degree in fashion promotion or fashion marketing, offered by several UK universities, could be an asset in gaining this type of job. The London College of Fashion's BA (Hons) Fashion Promotion course incorporates a specialist PR pathway.

The career route to PR normally starts with a work placement. The would-be PR could then possibly secure a job as an account handler. There are several alternative routes into PR: individuals with ambitions to work in PR may organise parties, model, be journalists or take part in anything hip and social in order to gain the essential contacts to become a PR. Fashion PRs are also lucky as they are part of one of the more commercial parts of the creative media industry. Many fashion PRs join recruitment agencies who help secure job interviews at prestigious firms. The best way to find out which recruitment agencies to approach is by word of mouth. For those lacking contacts within the fashion industry it is feasible to ring up established PR agencies and enquire which recruitment agencies they use.

PRs often go on to have a second career, helped by the contacts they have built up with their first agency. Some PRs move on to set up their own agencies or act as freelance PRs. In these circumstances PRs often take clients from their previous agencies with whom they have built up a good rapport which does not always leave a positive relationship with the previous PR agencies. Other possible careers PR can lead on to include fashion consultancy and journalism.

As with most fashion jobs PR titles and their meanings vary; it is up to each agency's discretion to decide exactly what their titles dictate. However the information below can be used as quite an accurate guide of what to expect.

Account handler/press assistant

This is an entry level role and involves supporting a PR account team. The main focus and responsibility at this level is administrative. Daily tasks may include packaging up and sending out clothes, sorting out press cuttings and chasing late sample returns. An ambitious PR will expect to occupy this role for a three to twelve month duration before looking for promotion. At this level the PR will have very little real interaction with the press so promotion usually depends on a convincing show of enthusiasm and drive.

Junior account executive

The junior account executive is responsible for all the press that appears in the lower end publications. This normally includes the tabloids and teenage magazines. In this role the PR builds relationships with journalists who work on these titles, suggesting feature ideas, writing press releases and facilitating the loan of relevant samples.

Account executive

This position is normally only awarded to PRs with a minimum of two to three years experience. The role is similar to that of a junior account executive but responsibility is increased as the PR is now dealing with the glossier publications and more prominent journalists. To reflect the increased value of the PR's relationship to the more established journalists they may be given expenses to help consolidate these contacts.

Account manager

An account manager is usually given this title after four to six years experience as an account executive. Account managers enjoy more responsibility, and are normally expected to start to take control of budgets for the accounts they manage. At this level there also comes the added pressure of an expectation that the PR may start to secure new clients.

Account director

Account directors usually have a minimum of six years experience and are capable of running the entire PR department. The PR has now progressed to a much more managerial and decision-making position, no longer playing such a big part in the day-to-day running of the company. Account directors now rely on the team to inform them of client coverage. In turn, the director has a much closer relationship with clients and may help them steer the direction of both their brand identity and press coverage.

Associate director/partner

This is very much a supervisory and figurehead role. Associate directors ensure that the whole team is running smoothly and are instrumental in hiring, firing and promotions. The directors also deal directly with the most important clients and journalists.

CASE STUDY

In-house PR for a retailer

Rebecca Smith is the senior press officer at Harrods. She joined the company in 2003 as the assistant press officer and was then promoted after a year when her boss left. Before taking on her role at Harrods Rebecca worked at the PR agency Brower Lewis for a year, where her position was press assistant.

Role and responsibilities

Rebecca enjoys the very prestigious job of working as the in-house PR for Harrods. Despite the fact she effectively works for one client, her role is very varied:

> *I am responsible for building consumer and media awareness of all the new and exclusive fashion which Harrods stocks. I write the press releases, photo call notices and oversee all the product placement in the national press. I also have to monitor and evaluate all the editorial coverage. This means looking through all the papers and checking where Harrods is featured and that the coverage is appropriate.*

Rebecca outlines what she enjoys most about working in fashion PR:

I love the fast pace and continuous change of the fashion industry and the opportunity to work on diverse and interesting projects and events. I relish the challenge of generating and placing effective press coverage. I also enjoy regularly meeting new and interesting people.

Rebecca neatly sums up how sophisticated communication skills are key to a successful career in public relations:

Communication skills are essential to work in public relations. Ultimately you are responsible for delivering the company brand image/message to the media. As well as speaking to and developing relationships with the press I also produce written material to promote any new fashion products, launches or events at Harrods.

Fashion PR is a very competitive arena, with the most glamorous jobs being chased by numerous capable applicants. Different employees have different criteria that make one applicant stand out from another. However it is safe to say that no single employer in fashion PR would argue with Rebecca's very practical advice.

Undertake as much hands on work experience as possible, even if this means doing unpaid placements. In this business making contacts and learning from people is absolutely invaluable.

FURTHER READING

Books

Costantino, M. (1998) *Marketing and PR: From Product Branding to Catwalk Show.* BT Batsford Ltd, London.

Kitchen, P.J. (1997) *Public Relations and Practice.* Thomson Learning, London.

Harrison, S. (2000) *Public Relations: An Introduction.* Thomson Learning, London.

Fashion journalism

By Helen Kenny

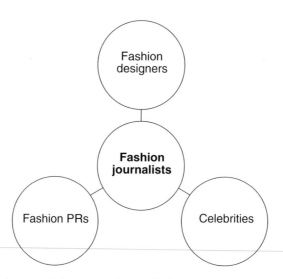

Fig. 14.1 Liaison between fashion journalists and other roles

Fashion journalism is concerned with communicating information about the fashion industry to the general public. There are three main media in which fashion journalists work: print, the internet and broadcast. All three forms of media require an exceptional grasp of the English language and an ability to articulate in an entertaining and informed manner; be it oral or written. This chapter focuses on print journalism as this is the biggest employment sector in the arena. Fashion journalism is one of the more competitive areas of the fashion industry. The majority of fashion journalists have completed a stint of unpaid work experience and published articles for little or no fee before landing a full-time job. Despite the odds, more and more young individuals are choosing to try to break into fashion journalism. The lure is strong; status, glamour, mixing with the rich and famous, and of course seeing your name and opinions in print.

It is impossible to overestimate the opportunities that the 'right' job title can create. Titles serve to communicate a journalist's status and significance to the rest of the industry. They let all the other fashion journalists know just how important the journalist in question is, and secure access to and determine seating at the fashion shows. Titles are also crucial for securing freelance and consultancy work and as a pathway to a journalist's next job. It is very difficult to pin down exact job titles and what they mean. This is because different magazines and newspapers use titles in different ways.

Sometimes titles are used as an appeasement measure when a journalist does not receive a much wanted pay rise. Below is an explanation of different sectors of fashion journalism. This is followed by a model that can be used as a 'blueprint' of titles and their meanings, which should fit most publications. The model also provides a good introduction to the various opportunities and roles that exist within the field of fashion journalism.

FASHION JOURNALISM IN MAGAZINES AND NEWSPAPERS

Once journalists establish that they would like to work in print there are certain decisions they have to make. Do they want to work for magazines or newspapers? Do they want to be 'character' journalists or more serious fashion commentators? Character journalists are known more for their opinions and advice than serious fashion commentary. These roles are not entirely mutually exclusive and journalists may play more than one role in the course of their careers. The vast majority of fashion journalists have to take their opportunities wherever they can find them. However, there are significant differences between working on a magazine or a newspaper. Magazine journalists have to answer more directly to their advertisers. Magazines for the large part are run and survive by their advertising revenue. This means that journalists writing for magazines have less freedom in the opinions they express. If a magazine condones an opinion that in some way is detrimental to the image of one of its advertisers it is not going to keep that advertiser very long.

In the trade press, such as *Drapers*, the writing is generally more objective and factual in style, though senior journalists often have the freedom to express their opinions on topical issues. They are less beholden to their advertisers as the editorial usually far outweighs advertising content. Fashion editors in the trade press are also invited to international fashion shows, like their counterparts in magazines aimed at the public. Trade press journalists require experience and contacts within the industry as the articles they write are aimed mainly at buyers, technologists and designers in retailers, brands and manufacturers.

In theory, newspapers do not answer to fashion advertisers and so the editorial contained in them is seen as possessing more integrity. It is, however, worth bearing in mind that any journalist, working for a newspaper or magazine, who criticises a designer risks being banned from future shows. There can be significant differences in the workload on a newspaper and a magazine. On a daily newspaper a fashion editor may be churning out a story a day and editing several others. On a monthly publication a fashion editor may write as little as one story a month and edit several others.

INTERNET JOURNALISM

Internet journalism provides a good source of income and an inroad for new journalists. A lot of freelance journalists pursue internet journalism as it provides a source of revenue and allows them to undertake lower paid but more high-status print journalism. Internet journalism has a better reputation when attached to an established and prestigious print publication such as vogue.co.uk. However, most of the journalists who write for these sites are already experienced and well-known print journalists. The internet also provides a useful vehicle for controversial journalism and gossip sites such as hintmag.co.uk are very popular with industry insiders. There are several fashion orientated websites which employ teams of journalists, including the subscription-only fashion forecasting and information site wgsn.com (see Chapter 3).

BROADCAST JOURNALISM

Broadcast journalism can refer to terrestrial or satellite television and radio. Broadcasting is a regular part of most prominent fashion journalists' jobs. Appearing as an authority on style programmes, both on television and radio, is a regular occurrence for many journalists. This is beneficial as it raises their profile and the publication for which the journalist works also gains free publicity. Most journalists actively participate in broadcast, but it is not usually a mandatory part of their career and some journalists decline to be involved. Broadcast journalism is a career that some journalists consider when moving on from the print sector: before Trinny and Susannah became known for telling the nation 'What Not To Wear' they wrote for *The Daily Telegraph*.

FREELANCE AND STAFF JOBS

A freelance fashion journalist is a self-employed writer who is not exclusively contracted to one publication (see Chapter 17). A staff job refers to employment exclusively on one publication. Few fashion journalists prefer to be exclusively freelance. When contracted to a staff job journalists normally enjoy the privilege of freelancing for other publications. The only exception to this is when the freelance contributions clash with the interests of the publication that the journalist is contracted to. The same restrictions unofficially apply to most freelancers. Journalists who start freelancing for two rival publications will normally soon find that neither will employ them.

Some generalisations can be made about fashion journalists' pay scales. Magazines tend to pay less than newspapers; the more commercial the title the better the pay; regional journalism pays less well than the nationals. Just as there is no linear career path for fashion journalists there is no linear wage scale. Staff journalists who are offered the opportunity to work on rival publications are normally offered more money in a bid to keep them at their current publication. Likewise there is no fixed rate for freelancers. Publications may expect articles to be submitted for no fee, particularly for unknown writers. In contrast, a well known journalist may easily command over a pound a word.

WHAT MAKES A FASHION JOURNALIST?

Certain personality characteristics help particular individuals to succeed when working in this sector of the industry. The primary characteristics are a complete passion for fashion, a conviction and belief in the importance of fashion and a love of beautiful design. Fashion journalists need to be exceptionally strong-minded and determined, with the ability to work very hard. They also need to be exceptionally gifted in dealing with complex people and politics. Competition is fierce for jobs; hierarchy and politics are both central and unavoidable in this arena. As soon as a job becomes available applications come flooding in. In reality most jobs are granted to people who come with personal recommendations. In this part of the industry a CV is not as important as a person's 'name' or reputation. This means that an ability to network and a very sociable personality are vital. Successful applicants can then work very long hours for demanding editors.

A fashion journalist requires a flexible personality and an ability to cope with uncertainty and change. There is not much job security in the world of fashion journalism. Job descriptions tend to be vague and contracts often have clauses which mean responsibilities can change at a moment's notice. There is no such thing as a typical day in fashion journalism. One day the job might involve interviewing Paul Smith and the next day road-testing the latest fashions in a local wine bar.

CAREER ROUTES

There is no one set route into fashion journalism. A good foundation of fashion knowledge gives any would-be fashion journalist a head start. This can be learnt either on a fashion course or through general interest. A degree with mainly written coursework, whether or not it is related to fashion or journalism, is preferable as it gives plenty of practice in writing skills. Surrey Institute offers the only BA (Hons) Fashion Journalism course in the UK.

Entry-level jobs in fashion journalism tend to entail a lot of mundane and routine work. The entry point normally entails a work placement or lots of unpaid or low-paid freelancing. Competition for work experience is fierce; it is a good idea to apply up to six months ahead for placements. An essential part of a journalist's career is establishing contacts and building working relationships. This means that the longer the work placement a trainee journalist can secure the better. Also, rather than trying to freelance for everyone it is best to build and nurture a few strong working relationships with key editors.

Fashion journalism is not only one of the most competitive areas of the fashion industry, it is also one of the most competitive parts of the journalism sector. So for some the route into fashion journalism might come through other avenues. A potential starting point for fashion journalists is in fashion PR as this allows one to build useful contacts (see Chapter 13). Fashion journalism is generally a young person's profession. For this reason fashion journalists often move on to related careers which can include fashion consultancy, PR, magazine editorship, setting up small fashion businesses and teaching. For example, Luella Bartley was a fashion writer who set up her own very influential designer label. The titles discussed below are very similar in terminology to titles discussed in Chapter 15 on fashion styling. This is because they are two complementary sides of the same coin. Due to the difference in tasks and responsibilities it is worth carefully considering how the titles take on different meanings depending on their context.

Fashion features assistant/fashion assistant

The fashion features assistant completes all the mundane tasks that keep the fashion team running. There are several different types of fashion assistants. Assistants who work on the features side of the fashion department are responsible for a variety of different tasks: chasing quotes, speaking to celebrities' agents to arrange interviews, chasing pictures to illustrate articles and numerous other tasks that keep a fashion department running.

Fashion writer

The fashion writer provides copy on all areas of fashion. A fashion writer is considered accomplished enough to provide articles and be a fashion authority, but is not senior enough to lead a team. They also enjoy prime positions at the shows.

Contributing fashion editor

This title refers to a journalist who has a contract with the publication yet is not a full-time member of staff. The contributing editor normally writes significant fashion articles. These could be show reports, designer interviews or current topical issues. Contributors are also valued for their general input into the publication and their status within the industry. In the case of more commercial publications, contributing fashion editors have a written contract and salary attached.

Independent publications may simply have verbal agreements and in some cases no fees attached.

Fashion features director/editor

The fashion features director presides over all the other fashion journalists on a publication and is instrumental in determining the course and tone of all fashion writing contained within the publication. This is not the limit of their responsibilities: directors also write the major fashion articles, conduct high-profile fashion interviews, advise the editor on recruitment in the fashion team, submit relevant cover lines and attend the international fashion shows.

Deputy fashion editor

The job of the deputy is to support the fashion editor, helping with general editing duties, suggesting feature ideas, completing the bulk of the writing and also attending the fashion shows.

Fashion editor

There may be several fashion editors on a title. The fashion editor's job is very similar to the fashion features director's job. The difference to a certain degree lies in the significance of the title. A fashion features director has a certain level of status within the fashion community. The fashion editor executes very similar tasks yet is not considered to have quite enough knowledge or contacts to merit the title of director.

CASE STUDY

Fashion director of a newspaper

Career path

Hilary Alexander is the fashion director at *The Daily Telegraph*. Hilary completed a three-year apprenticeship on newspapers in New Zealand, where she was born. She then worked on various newspapers in Hong Kong, Australia and New Zealand. She worked for the Hong Kong Trade Development Council as fashion editor and was responsible for the twice yearly *Apparel* magazine. This job had many aspects which included writing press releases on Hong Kong's fashion industry, assisting the organisation of the press campaigning behind the ready-to-wear festival and launching and organising the Hong Kong Young Designers' Show. Hilary took over from Kathryn Samuel at *The Daily Telegraph*. Kathryn was of the old school fashion brigade and everyone called her 'Ma'am'. In contrast, Hilary is of the new guard and is thoroughly unpretentious and modern – she gets called Hils. She once persuaded Karl Lagerfeld to waltz her around his Paris lawn wearing green wellies.

Role and responsibilities

Hilary first joined *The Daily Telegraph* in January 1985. Today she is a well known and iconic figure in the world of fashion journalism. From 1985 to date she has worked herself up the ranks. Hilary started off as a fashion writer, graduated to deputy fashion editor and is now the fashion director. This is unusual in that most writers and stylists tend to have to move publications to be promoted. This can involve long stretches of precarious freelance or moving to a less prestigious publication to gain a higher salary or a grander title. Hilary's responsibilities are many and varied:

> *My main responsibilities include styling and shooting the main Monday fashion page; writing and styling pieces for the Style-Fashion section on Wednesdays; writing the weekly 'Ask Hilary' column; providing news stories whenever any fashion news happens and providing news coverage of the ready-to-wear shows in London, New York, Milan, Paris and the* haute couture *shows in Paris.*

Hilary's job description is open ended and no day comes with a set script and list of jobs to do. She is also responsible for providing topical-led Saturday stories when needed in addition to interviews and make-overs with rock stars and celebrities. Travel is no small part of her job:

> *Twice a year I go to New York, Milan and Paris for the catwalk shows and to Paris for the* haute couture *shows. At least four times a year I organise overseas shoots. This year, at the time of writing it is November, I have had shoots in Mauritius, Kazakhstan, Mongolia, Morocco and Dubrovnik so far. Usually when I am travelling I also try to provide a travel/fashion story for the travel section.*

The multi-tasking and dexterity behind the job are not confined to the numerous demands of the day's various tasks and deadlines. Hilary also has to juggle working on two and sometimes three seasons simultaneously. This is because the catwalk shows are six months ahead of what is sold in the shops. So Hilary is seeing one season on the catwalk and filing news reports on the trends, whilst also submitting shoots and copy for the season that is currently in store.

Fashion journalists communicate information and their perspective to the public. Hilary sees communication skills as:

> *Vital – we spend so much time on the telephone, on e-mail in order to request samples and find out about stories. Communication is an integral part of interviewing people for news and feature stories.*

Hilary communicates using various different media. As well as contributing to *The Daily Telegraph* she contributes to *The Telegraph online* www.telegraph.co.uk and various different television channels. As Hilary modestly puts it:

I do a bit of television, ranging from resident styling to quick sound bites after shows or in-depth interviews on specific subjects. I was the resident stylist on **Britain's Next Top Model,** *a series shown on Living TV. I also regularly appear on BBC Breakfast, CNN, GMTV and all the main cable channels including Fashion File, Video Fashion and channels all around the world including Germany, Russia, Croatia and Poland.*

Before Hilary puts anything to press she has to liaise and communicate with various people in the fashion industry. These range from PRs, to photographers, stylists, make-up artists and hair stylists. Hilary has the difficult job of interviewing designers, who quite often live up to their stereotype of egocentric, insecure prima donnas, and to extract information from these personalities the most delicate and subtle communication skills are needed. As most newspaper fashion journalists, Hilary does not work in isolation from the rest of the newspaper. There is constant cross-referencing with all departments: news, picture desk, travel, features and even obituaries and motoring. As Hilary sums up: 'teamwork is crucial – without it nothing would happen'.

Even the most glamorous jobs have their downsides. Hilary neatly and poignantly sums up her perceived perception of the effect of her commitment to a demanding career:

Most difficult is accepting that I have little or no personal life. Travelling, work schedules, etc. preclude a serious relationship and sadly it also means I cannot have a cat – and I adore cats. The moment I retire I will have three cats at least!

Hilary is a unique individual who has a very strong passion for her chosen vocation, but what drives her?

All of it – I love travelling, love writing, love styling, love people, clothes, accessories, the shops, the show rooms – everything! I can't imagine a better job.

Career advice

As stated earlier in the chapter, fashion journalism is a demanding and intensely competitive career. Hilary Alexander has managed to rise to the top of this profession. Here are her invaluable words of advice for anyone considering a career in fashion journalism:

Be bright, enthusiastic, love what you do, have good command of spoken and written English, not mind long hours and be prepared for hard work.

FURTHER READING

Books

Brubach, H. (1999) *Dedicated Follower of Fashion.* Phaidon, London.
Oppenheimer, J. (2004) *Front Row: Anna Wintour.* Saint Martin's Press, London.

Vreeland, D. (2001) *Why Don't You . . . ? Audacious Advice for Fashionable Living: Diana Vreeland, the 'Bazaar' Years*. Universe Publishing, New York.
Watt, J. (1999) *The Penguin Book of Twentieth Century Fashion Writing*. Penguin, London.

Magazines

Another Magazine
Dazed & Confused
Drapers
Elle
Glamour
Harpers Bazaar
I D
Pop
Tatler
Vogue (British, French, Italian and American editions)

Newspapers

International Herald Tribune
The Daily Telegraph
The Independent
The Sunday Times

Websites

www.hintmag.com
www.style.com
www.vogue.co.uk

Fashion styling

By Helen Kenny

Fig. 15.1 Liaison between fashion stylists and other roles

The roles of fashion stylists are many and varied. Traditionally the term fashion styling refers to choosing clothes and putting together looks for the purpose of a catwalk show or fashion shoot. In an ever more image-conscious world the role of the fashion stylist has expanded. Nowadays it is possible to find fashion stylists working in conjunction with advertising executives, music stars, celebrities or members of the general public. During their careers, fashion stylists find themselves undertaking most, if not all, of these roles.

153

EDITORIAL, CATALOGUE AND ADVERTISING

It is in editorial, catalogues and advertising, that most styling takes place. Editorial, in the context of fashion magazines, refers to the pages in the magazine that reflect the opinion or vision of the editor, the publisher or in this case the stylist. This makes an editorial role an important one for a stylist and it is the primary vehicle for creative expression. In terms of making a name and winning kudos and status, editorial is the cornerstone of the stylist's career development. Financially, editorial work is less appealing; it is not usually as well-paid as advertising or catalogue work. Being a regular contributor to magazines can make a very satisfactory living for a stylist. Most editorial stylists, whether freelance or on staff contracts, supplement their income with catalogue and advertising work.

Catalogues exist to display or list information. In the case of fashion catalogues the information is clothing and accessories. The nature of catalogues means that stylists have less creative freedom in their work than in magazines. Some stylists specialise in catalogues and advertising but there is a limit to how far their careers can progress; a healthy and lucrative living can be made but a certain status and access within the fashion industry is denied to the stylist. As the primary purpose of the fashion catalogue is to convey information it is inevitable that aesthetic sensibility comes second. This means working for catalogues gives the stylists little artistic kudos. Most catalogues deal with own label ranges, brands and diffusion collections so there is no reason for the catalogue stylist to attend or be invited to the prestigious designer and couture shows. It is at these shows that many important working relationships are made and consolidated.

All advertising work is concerned with capturing the potential purchaser's attention. The stylist may undertake advertising for less highly-regarded brands or campaigns if they are financially lucrative. A campaign for an influential brand or label is beneficial to the stylist in terms of status and the money it pays.

WHAT MAKES A SUCCESSFUL FASHION STYLIST?

Fashion stylists need to possess a developed aesthetic sense, creative flair and a very wide range of visual knowledge and references. This can be built up by visiting museums and galleries, watching films, looking at vintage magazines and reading books about fashion history. Fashion stylists also need to possess an ability to cope with rejection, and to be able to work incredibly varied long hours. This is not a job for those who like to work regular hours.

PREPPING AND DIRECTING THE SHOOT

The majority of fashion styling is concerned with arranging clothes as attractively as possible for the purpose of a photographic shoot. This may be for the purpose of conveying information, for aesthetic entertainment or both. The most challenging fashion shoots may help construct a brand image, challenge existing conventions, employ subversive humour or simply show the most sophisticated interpretation of the current seasons' trends. To produce a fashion image a team of individuals, each with their own defined roles, is used. Typically this team consists of at least five individuals: the photographer, stylist, model, hair and make-up artist. There are numerous differences between editorial, catalogue and advertising shoots. Consequently editorial shoots are discussed separately within the chapter, followed by catalogue and advertising shoots, which share more in common.

The magazine shoot

The stylist and photographer are normally in charge of the artistic vision behind the shoot; although they have to work to the brief set by the client. Once the stylist has a particular shoot in mind they source the clothes and book the team. It is normally the responsibility of the stylist to ensure that the team is in place. The photographer may request, or if he or she is very eminent insist, on certain hairstylists or make up artists or models being used. The photographer does not normally expect to book or organise the team, however. If the stylist is lucky enough to have one or more assistants they will be given instructions and expected to chase the clothes and organise the team.

Organising shoots is always a juggling game; it is necessary to choose the desired team for the shoot, and this is a delicate decision. Some photographers are known to be difficult to work with and sometimes publications ban using certain photographers. New stylists need to concentrate on building relationships with a few key people who are going to give them access to this complicated hierarchy. It is a good idea to build relationships with friendly bookers. Bookers are the photographers' and models' agents and so are very influential in persuading clients to use photographic and modelling agencies. They recommend the new blood to work with fashion stylists. The ambitious new stylist targets the most prestigious agencies. These agencies have 'floaters' on their books: new talents who show great promise but are not yet established enough to be taken on by the agency. In modelling agencies the less-established models are part of the division called 'new faces'.

The shoot is the product of weeks or even months of work. The research for the shoot might have included seeing the season's shows, going on showroom appointments, sourcing new designer talent, scouring vintage markets, watching relevant films and visiting exhibitions. On the day of the shoot the fashion team will turn up at a set location and time which will be written on the call sheet. The call sheet details the shoot location, time, story name and the names of everyone taking part in the shoot. The shoot may be on location, which could be down the road or on the other side of the world, or maybe in a studio. The average shoot takes place in a single day. However, more elaborate shoots may happen over days or even weeks. The shoot starts with a discussion of the mood and character that the stylist is trying to create. This discussion primarily takes place between the photographer and stylist who then brief the hair and make-up artists. There is a break while the photographer sets up the lights and the hair and make-up artists prepare the model. The stylist normally uses this time to help the assistant unpack the cases and steam the clothes. Once the shoot begins the stylist has to dress the models and keep an eye on the clothes while they are being photographed.

Catalogue and advertising shoots

As discussed earlier in the chapter, catalogue and most advertising work allows the stylist far less creative freedom than editorial work. On both catalogue and advertising shoots it is standard practice to employ an art director. The art director will then often dictate how the shoot progresses. The art director will have organised the photographer, location, hair and make up, model and clothes. The stylist may simply have the job of selecting combinations of clothes or if the art director has pre-selected the combinations the stylist may simply be steaming and pinning the clothes.

Catwalk shows

The most successful stylists also style catwalk shows. How involved the stylist is with the vision behind the show and the design process beforehand depends on the relationship with the designer. The most trusted and respected stylists may be involved from the initial ideas behind the collection to casting and dressing the models for the show.

CAREER ROUTES

There are various routes into the competitive world of fashion styling. Before securing an entry-level job most individuals complete unpaid work placements on magazines or assist a freelance stylist for little or no fee. Would-be stylists can also work their way into the industry by using alternative methods to make contacts; by working in a styling/photographic agency, working as a model or even hosting events or parties. An assistant has to undertake a large number of tests before becoming established as a stylist. A test refers to a shoot which has not been commissioned and is undertaken to build a stylist's portfolio or to be shown to magazine editors in an effort to get the shoot published, in which case valuable tear sheets for the stylist's portfolio are provided. Tear sheets refer to pages from magazines on which the stylist's work is printed. Once a number of tears has been amassed the assistant works on establishing a freelance career as a fashion stylist or landing a more permanent job.

The life of a fashion stylist can be precarious with little job security. Those lucky enough to land a job on a magazine are under constant pressure to be the 'hottest' to maintain their positions. Financial rewards are not set on a linear scale, either for a freelance or staff job. To a large extent the amount stylists are paid depends on the currency of their name. Most fashion stylists are relatively young and many stylists go on to pursue second careers. These careers cover a wide range and may include fashion photography, PR, lecturing, designing and other areas of the fashion industry.

Most of the titles discussed below refer to fashion styling for magazines. This is because fashion magazines have very hierarchical structures (see Chapter 14 for more explanation of job roles on magazines). It is worth noting how responsibilities change, under similar tiles, when dealing with the visual responsibilities of fashion styling as opposed to the fashion journalist who is concerned with the written word. Freelance, celebrity and music stylists tend to work alone or with between one and three assistants. Personal stylists almost always work individually.

Fashion director

This is a title very few stylists achieve; the fashion director leads the magazine's fashion team in terms of visual direction and interpreting the *Zeitgeist*. The fashion director also enjoys a certain status within the closed world of the fashion media. This is a status that normally exists prior to and aids the stylist's promotion to fashion director. Stylists who become fashion directors will of necessity have already earned a respected name in the fashion world for their work.

Senior fashion editor/fashion editor

The fashion editor enjoys a powerful position on the fashion team. They shoot the ready-to-wear stories and may also shoot couture stories. There may be several fashion editors on a publication. The editors also supervise the more junior members of the fashion team.

Junior/deputy fashion editor

The junior fashion editor's job is normally the stepping stone between being a fashion assistant and a fashion editor. The Junior Fashion Editor shoots the mass market and middle market shoots: high street stores, fashion brands and the cheaper diffusion labels.

Contributing fashion editor

This title refers to a stylist who makes a significant contribution to a publication. As recognition of this contribution the stylist is awarded a contributor's contract and the above title which formally acknowledges their role for the publication. Contributors bring two separate things to a publication in order to earn this title; they submit a substantial number of significant shoots and their names also have a certain cachet in the industry which will benefit the publication.

Fashion assistant

Fashion assistants complete all the mundane tasks that keep the team running. They fax, e-mail or telephone requests for clothes and chase bookings on hair, make-up, models and studios. The fashion assistant participates in fashion shoots, helping with packing and carrying the cases and with the dressing of the model.

Assistant to the fashion director

The assistant to the fashion director is a very privileged fashion assistant working with the most important person on the fashion team. This position is unique in that the assistant's loyalty often lies more with the fashion director than the publication they both work for. This means that if the fashion director moves publication, the assistant tends to follow.

Freelance fashion stylist

This term refers primarily to a stylist who does not hold an exclusive contract with any publication or person. These stylists may work with magazines, catalogues, advertising, celebrities or members of the public. The main defining factor is they do not have one employer they are obliged to answer to but work on individual contracts as the opportunity arises (see Chapter 17).

Celebrity stylist

A number of stylists work almost exclusively with celebrities. Unsurprisingly, the most lucrative of these stylists are based in LA. Their clients may include television presenters, actors, singers and musicians. The celebrity stylists attend or keep up-to-date with the fashion shows; they then use their very current fashion knowledge in varying ways. They may dress their clients for the entire season ahead, and in the case of a very demanding client, be almost constantly on call, or they may only dress their client for special occasions which could range from an appearance on a chat show to a night at the Oscars.

Music stylists

There are stylists who only work with music clients. If they have a very established client they may only need to work with one person. It is not unusual for editorial stylists to also have music clients.

Personal stylist

To a certain extent the personal stylist has a similar role to the celebrity stylist. Both types deal with their clients on a one-to-one basis and are in charge of the client's fashion image. The personal stylist's clients are not well-known and have different demands; their own image is not so important as they do not live so much in the public eye. This means that most personal stylists normally help their clients build confidence to develop their own style.

CASE STUDY

Fashion assistant for a magazine

Career path

Mary Fellowes has been a fashion assistant at *British Vogue* since 2003 (see Fig. 15.2). She studied BA (Hons) Fashion (communications) then worked for the *Evening Standard ES* magazine in London as a fashion assistant and assisted various stylists, including the renowned Isabella Blow.

Role and responsibilities

Working for Britain's premier fashion publication is no small responsibility. Mary outlines the main responsibilities of her job:

> *I am responsible for sourcing new talents and interesting pieces, liaising with press officers to be aware of new collections, calling in clothes and accessories for shoots and, of course, seeing fashion shows.*

Mary realises that a job on *Vogue* is most young fashionistas' dream. However, she points out that as with any other job there are downsides:

> *We have to deal with the stress of multi-tasking, the necessary ultra-efficient attitude to organisation, multi-tasking, the politics of the office and heartbreakingly not having enough time to support new talent.*

Mary is quick to point out how lucky she feels to have this unique job and lists the many enjoyable aspects:

> *I love the travel, the creativity, using my initiative and seeing my ideas in the publication. It is also amazing to see the effect you can have on the big production fashion shoots. Another huge perk is meeting tons of interesting people who have long been my heroes – for example Mario Testino and Nick Knight.*

Mary spells out the importance of teamwork and communication in a stylist's job:

> *Teamwork is highly important, on shoots and in ensuring that we all have different showroom engagements and cover all the appointments. Also in ensuring that the clothes are efficiently and safely returned.*

Communication is vital to a stylist's success and Mary explains why this is so:

> *The more professional and friendly your telephone manner the more likely you are to receive the samples you request. This is crucial when you have stylists and assistants*

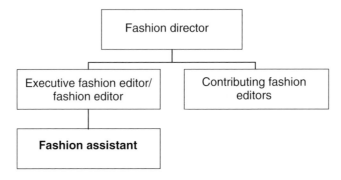

Fig. 15.2 Structure of the fashion team at British Vogue

all over the world chasing the 'hot' piece of the season. Magazines are finely tuned places and it is crucial to communicate fully with the team about 'where you are at' and how the shoot you are prepping is progressing.

Mary offers some very sensible advice for the would-be stylist:

Be individual, work very hard indeed, use masses of initiative, be proactive and be interested.

FURTHER READING

Books

Coddington, G. (2002) *Grace: Thirty Years of Fashion at 'Vogue'*. Steidl, London.
Dingemanns, J. (1999) *Mastering Fashion Styling*. Palgrave Macmillan, Hampshire.
Sherrill, M. and Karmel, C.A. (2002) *Stylemakers: Inside Fashion*. Monacelli, New York.
Vreeland, D. (2003) *D.V.* Da Capo Press.

Fashion and textiles education **16**

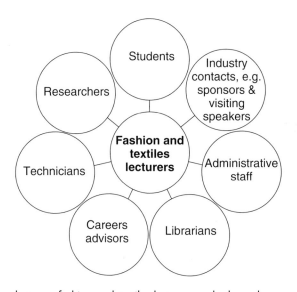

Fig. 16.1 Liaison between fashion and textiles lecturers and other roles

This chapter covers fashion and textiles education as a career choice for graduates. The courses covered can also be considered as study options for potential students of fashion and textiles. Lecturers have the opportunity to impart a wide selection of skills and knowledge gained through experience of working and studying in their field to future generations of practitioners. Although contact time with students through various teaching methods is a significant part of most lecturers' work, other duties constitute the majority of a full-time lecturer's contracted hours including:

- teaching preparation;
- assessment;

- course administration;
- staff development and research.

   To become a lecturer in fashion or textiles it is necessary to have experience and knowledge in a relevant area. Lecturers can work in either the Higher Education sector (HE) which consists almost exclusively of students who are aged 18 or over or in Further Education (FE) in which students are mainly 16–19 years old. Teaching is frequently viewed as an attractive option in terms of its generous holiday allowance, though full-time lecturers work during most of their students' vacation.

HIGHER EDUCATION

Most fashion and textiles-related subjects are offered at degree level: a Bachelor of Arts (BA) for design-orientated courses or Bachelor of Science (BSc) for more technical subjects, usually located in the Art and Design faculty of a university or other HE institution. Relevant degree subjects for different types of job in fashion and textiles are mentioned in the preceding chapters. Many degree courses take students directly after A-levels but some design courses also request an art foundation course, which is a one-year course studied at either an FE or HE institution. At least one A-level in art, textiles or another creative subject is desirable, though not always essential, in applicants for fashion or textiles-related degrees. Foundation degrees and BTEC HNDs are similar to each other as they are vocational HE courses studied two years full-time or three years if taken as a sandwich course and it is possible to progress from one of these courses into the second or third year of an appropriate BA (Hons) degree. Most degrees are three years in duration, but some universities offer a four-year sandwich course, including up to a year working in industry. This is often viewed as an asset by employers as it gives undergraduates experience of how the industry operates in practice.

   Most design-orientated HE courses request a portfolio of work which should include the applicant's best work, with the emphasis much more on quality than quantity. In degree applicants lecturers look for potential in students demonstrated by finalised work supported by sheets of development ideas or sketchbooks and a clear indication of the interviewee's drawing skills. Applicants are sometimes advised to develop projects with design ideas aimed at a selected store and range of products within a portfolio and lecturers may set a brief for interview candidates. It is important for potential students to discuss and explain the thought process behind their ideas in interviews.

Postgraduate education

After taking a first degree, i.e. BA or BSc, it is possible for graduates to progress to a postgraduate master's course in a related subject such as an MA or MSc, with one to two years study full-time, or longer on a part-time basis. Masters' degrees are becoming increasingly important as the number of graduates is rising and many are pursuing this level of study to set themselves apart from their competitors in the jobs market. Having a master's degree does not necessarily provide entry to a higher level of job or a better salary than a bachelor's degree but gives the student the opportunity to explore a subject in more depth. Qualifications in teaching or postgraduate studies are not compulsory for all lecturers, but are often advantageous. A postgraduate certificate in education (PGCE) is a one-year full-time course for primary and secondary school teaching but for FE or HE can be taken on a part-time basis by lecturers with a permanent post.

FURTHER EDUCATION

FE comprises colleges of FE, art colleges and sixth-form colleges which offer courses including GNVQs (which will be phased out by 2007), BTEC Nationals and A-levels. A BTEC National Diploma is a two-year course validated by Edexcel assessed through projects related to work situations, which is roughly equivalent to three A-levels. BTEC National Diplomas are offered in various art and design subjects including fashion and clothing, and with high pass grades it is possible to progress directly onto a degree. A BTEC National Award is equivalent to one A-level and can be studied alongside A-levels. Some FE colleges run HE courses which are validated by or franchised from universities. Many FE colleges and some HE institutions offer adult education courses at evening classes or in blocks during vacations which can provide supplementary skills to those working in the fashion and textiles industry.

SCHOOLS

Fashion and textiles graduates can become teachers in primary or secondary schools if they have relevant teaching qualifications, a minimum of two A levels (or equivalent) and grade C in GCSE english and maths. It is possible to teach general subjects, art, design and technology or textiles within schools. School teachers usually require 'qualified teaching status' (QTS) which they can gain from completing a PGCE. Whilst studying for a PGCE in primary or secondary education UK students are granted a tax-free training bursary of £6–9000 (in 2005). Some secondary school subjects including design and technology currently attract a 'golden hello' of £2500 at the start of the second year of teaching.

PART-TIME LECTURING

Part-time (or visiting) lecturers earn an hourly rate for their teaching contact hours. Part-time rates are generally higher in HE than in FE. Part-timers may also be paid for assessment and preparation, but they usually work only in term-time and are not generally involved with curriculum development, course management or administration tasks. The part-time lecturing rate is higher than the equivalent hourly rate that most full-time lecturers earn, but part-timers are expected to do much or all of the teaching preparation in their own time. Some lecturers work on a permanent *pro rata* contract for a set number of days per week for a proportionate salary, with the same types of administrative responsibilities as full-time lecturers.

LECTURING APPLICATION AND INTERVIEW PROCESS

Vacancies for lecturers in fashion and textiles are usually advertised in *Drapers*, *The Guardian* and jobs.ac.uk. Jobs in certain fashion-related posts may be advertised in a relevant trade publication to attract the appropriate calibre of applicants, e.g. a fashion marketing lecturing post could be featured in *Marketing Week*. Educational institutions frequently follow up references for the interviewees in advance, in contrast to industry where referees are usually contacted after the job has been offered to a candidate. A traditional format for interviewing lecturers is often used in both FE and HE, which is relatively formal and unusual in that competing candidates meet each other. The interview process for a full-time lecturer's position frequently includes at least one formal interview and a presentation which take place on the same day. This process usually starts with a tour of the teaching accommodation for all of the applicants together. Formal interviews with senior managers within the faculty may then be carried out with each of the candidates in turn. Interviewees are often asked to give a presentation to a panel of academics in the appropriate subject area in answer to a brief based on a fashion or textiles topic or a broader question relating to art and design education. This enables the panel to assess the applicant's teaching ability and capacity to work under pressure. In contrast, part-time lecturing jobs are rarely advertised. Part-time lecturers are not always interviewed and may be appointed because they are known by existing members of a course team or have submitted a speculative application.

LECTURING CONTRACTS AND RESPONSIBILITIES

Lecturers are usually given specific job titles and teach certain elements of one or more courses. Lecturers working on the same course at the same level may be asked to deliver distinctly different teaching content from each other. The lecturer's role is split between contact hours and administrative tasks relating to the development and delivery of courses, recruitment and staff development, with a notional number of hours attached to each part of the job. Teaching methods used in fashion and textiles vary depending on the subject and can include:

- formal lectures;
- seminars;
- tutorials;
- studio practice;
- workshops.

Teaching preparation can involve planning lecture content and setting projects with sponsors. In HE much of the communication with students relating to their courses can now take place through the use of an intranet to which staff and students have access, e.g. for relaying messages and lecture notes. Assessment is another key component of a lecturer's workload with feedback being given to students during the development of project work. Lecturers have to plan the criteria on which projects will be assessed (also known as learning outcomes) and use these when summative assessment is given at the end of a project with a grade or percentage. Lecturers are then usually responsible for inputting data to record these grades so that students' performance can be calculated. Lecturers are responsible for comparing projects within a module or course in a process known as moderation, to ensure that grades from different lecturers are comparable. External moderators are experienced lecturers from other educational institutions, and sometimes from industry, who review the standard of students' work within a course with the aim of ensuring consistent quality. Outside term-time, lecturers continue their non-teaching responsibilities.

COURSE MANAGEMENT AND ADMINISTRATION

In addition to teaching-related duties, lecturers on permanent contracts participate in many of the following course management and administrative duties:

- personal tutorials (pastoral) to a year group (cohort) of students;
- open days and university/college tours for prospective students;
- reviewing existing courses and developing new courses;
- course team meetings;
- promoting courses, e.g. at *Graduate Fashion Week* or *New Designers* exhibitions;
- membership of committees within the university;
- references for alumni (ex-students).

STAFF DEVELOPMENT AND RESEARCH

Staff development allows lecturers to expand their skills by taking part in short courses, usually in-house or at other universities, attending conferences and exhibitions and other relevant activities. HE lecturers are also expected to undertake 'scholarly activity' by reading about their subjects to remain up-to-date with contemporary developments. Lecturers have appraisals with their managers to discuss their progress and to identify relevant staff development and possible research opportunities. Research can form part of some lecturers' timetables, enabling them to gain in-depth, original information in a specialist subject area which can inform their peers and students and gain prestige for the educational institution. Funding can be acquired for research (mainly from government-funded research councils) and some academic roles include research on a full-time or part-time basis. Research outputs include publications, the presentation of papers at conferences and contributions towards exhibitions.

CAREER ROUTES

There are three levels of full-time lecturer grade, each with a different salary range:

- lecturer;
- senior lecturer;
- principal lecturer.

The salaries of each grade overlap with the next level and are based mainly on the lecturer's amount of experience. Lecturers' pay scales are very standardised compared to those in industry. They are generally the same throughout the UK and increase annually by a small amount relating to inflation plus a set yearly amount, known as an increment, which is capped at the top of the salary bracket. Lecturers' salaries generally tend to be lower than their counterparts at management level in industry, but this disadvantage can be offset by the relative security of a lecturing contract, holiday allowance and the job satisfaction of working with students. Most full-time fashion and textiles lecturers teach part-time initially as most universities and colleges rarely appoint lecturers without previous teaching experience. This creates difficulties for many people to make the move from industry into education as it is often impractical to teach part-time whilst working in a full-time post.

As well as extensive experience as a lecturer or in industry (or both) a principal lecturer usually has some significant extra responsibility to warrant a higher salary, such as being a subject leader or taking on additional high-profile promotional duties for the department. Course leaders, sometimes known as programme leaders, are mostly at senior lecturer level and take much of the responsibility for course administration and promotion, working alongside other lecturers. The term 'subject leader' can be used to describe a member of staff in charge of more than one degree course who is not as senior as a head of department. The middle and senior management positions within HE can vary within universities but are likely to be, in ascending order:

- head of department/academic team leader;
- associate dean;
- dean;

- pro-vice chancellor;
- vice-chancellor.

CASE STUDIES

University lecturer in fashion design

Career path

Christopher New is a senior lecturer at Central Saint Martins (CSM), responsible for running the BA (Hons) Fashion Design Menswear pathway, and is the academic tutor for student placements. After graduating with BSc (Hons) Biochemistry in 1980, then studying the subject at postgraduate level for two years, he decided to follow a similar route to his family, who owned a clothing factory, and began working in the fashion business. He worked for Paul Smith for three years then launched his own menswear label and store which he ran for 13 years. He subsequently designed for Japanese fashion labels and worked as a graphic designer before becoming a lecturer in 1997.

Role and responsibilities

Christopher lists his main responsibilities as:

- organising the menswear design curriculum;
- arranging student placements;
- organising visiting lecturers for the course;
- being the key lecturer for menswear design;
- administration;
- being a pastoral tutor;
- interviewing students (and occasionally lecturers);
- researching.

Christopher organises and develops the course content and invites visiting tutors to work with the students on specific subjects or projects. His line manager is the BA (Hons) Fashion Design course director (see Fig. 16.2) who reports to the Dean of the School of Fashion, Textiles and Jewellery. The course accepts a cohort of around 200 students per year over seven pathways, of which womenswear has the largest intake. Christopher takes on around 20 full-time menswear students each year for the three-year course, and there is an option to study it as a four-year sandwich course with a placement year. Technicians with pattern cutting, sewing or IT expertise are employed within the pathways to offer technical guidance to the students. Christopher explains how he works with administrators and other members of staff in the university:

> *Teamwork is extremely important. You need a support network and we have very good administrative support – because we have so many students we need to have that. I*

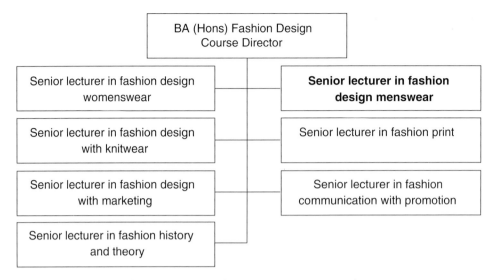

Fig. 16.2 Structure of the BA (Hons) Fashion Design team at Central Saint Martins

don't actually cross over that much with my colleagues who work on the other path-ways but they are there to discuss things, which is extremely valuable. Our course direc-tor is supportive too and oversees the pathways to make sure there's parity. The visiting tutors who come in are mainly designers working in the industry and do projects for three or four weeks for a few days per week. I liaise with them to make sure the whole thing runs smoothly.

Christopher travels within his job to visit fabric mills in Yorkshire and to see the menswear shows in Paris. He liaises with companies such as Paul Smith, Dunhill Menswear, coat manufacturer Gloverall and fabric suppliers for spon-sored projects whose input can vary from fabrics to money or valuable advice. His average working day is from 9.30AM to 7.30PM although these hours are bal-anced out by the fact that he has more holiday time than most other jobs would offer. Christopher studied to obtain teaching qualifications at the Centre for Learn-ing and Teaching in Art and Design and has also developed his IT skills on staff development courses:

I use computers a lot for admin. work, probably more than many of my colleagues. I use packages like Adobe Illustrator and Photoshop which are important for my students but also because I use them for designing. We officially have 20 per cent of our timetable to spend on our own research, which can be freelance, and I'm designing for a company that makes shirts.

Christopher also participated in a three-year research project called 'Fashion and Modernity' culminating in an exhibition at CSM in July 2004. He describes what he considers to be the main advantages and disadvantages of his job:

What gives me a real kick is seeing the way the students develop over a three-year period as they mature and their designing progresses. Watching them learn and improve over the years is what I find most rewarding and day-to-day I enjoy teaching projects. With all teaching now there has to be a lot of quality assurance and it generates a lot of admin. and paperwork which is necessary, but takes up a lot of time and can be arduous.

Career advice

Christopher explains the range of skills he looks for when appointing fashion lecturers:

You need patience to do this job because you're taking on a new set of students every year. You have to be innovative and try new things because you can't serve up the same projects every time, so you need to keep up with fashion. I look for people with really good communication skills who enjoy working with young people. You have to be able to get on with all the admin. which has to be done. You need to have worked in the industry first to be able to understand it before you become a lecturer. You might be able to design well but it's important to know all the other things that go with it. You need to make a decision that you're changing direction from being a fashion designer to go into lecturing. It's a more stable job with some nice long holidays and is a very rewarding career.

University lecturer in textile design

Career path

Dr Amanda Briggs-Goode is a Senior Lecturer in Textile Design at Nottingham Trent University (NTU). After graduating in BA (Hons) Design at Staffordshire University in 1988 she initially worked as a print designer for Courtaulds, then designed for Crown and has since done freelance work and commissions designing various products including ceramics, stationery, fashion and interiors. She completed an MA in Computing in Design at Middlesex University in 1992 before taking a PGCE/FE teaching course at the University of Greenwich and studying her PhD at NTU. She started teaching at NTU on a part-time basis before taking up a permanent post in 2001.

Role and responsibilities

Amanda specialises in teaching printed textiles and is also the research co-ordinator within the Applied Design academic team. Her main responsibilities include:

- course development;
- curriculum development;
- teaching textile design to undergraduate students;
- contributing to the 'design and visual culture' curriculum in lectures and dissertation supervision;
- supervising MA and PhD students;
- researching in printed textiles;

- course administration;
- course promotion and recruitment;
- interviewing course applicants.

Amanda reports to the academic team leader for applied design who also manages the BA (Hons) Fashion and Textile Management and BA (Hons) Fashion Knitwear Design and Knitted Textiles courses. Amanda describes how she works with her colleagues and students:

There are eight members of staff on the course team and about 180 students so we work in teams a lot to plan what we need to deliver and how we are going to do it. We often team-teach, particularly at first year level. The course demands a team approach, but this is sometimes at odds with an academic's agenda which is often about autonomy. Obviously when you work in a team it is important to be able to have good relationships with colleagues as we all depend on each other to a greater or lesser degree. It is important that you can communicate well with students and colleagues. This needs to be carefully balanced with being sensitive to students' needs on an individual basis. For example, in a lecture you are obviously talking to a group and can only think about a cohort. However, in a tutorial context you may need to think about how you communicate with individuals as some students will have different needs which demand different approaches.

Amanda helps to promote the course in various ways, through presentations to students and displays of work for university open days and national exhibitions such as *New Designers*. She and her colleagues run projects and competitions with several companies for the undergraduate students. In addition to lecturing duties she attends some of the regular staff development courses available through the university in subjects such as IT skills and new teaching methods. She plans her own research and says:

It's important to keep up-to-date with changes and new approaches in education. Scholarship and research are very important to your development, your currency as an individual and your teaching.

Amanda enjoys the teaching and research elements of her job most and she considers the most difficult aspects to be dealing with 'some students who do not engage with their learning' and administration, which she finds time-consuming. Her role involves a variable amount of travel in the UK and also some international trips, mainly to deliver research papers at conferences.

Career advice

Amanda regards the key requirements for those wanting to lecture in design to be:

- relevant qualifications;
- experience in design;
- an academic profile, i.e. research and teaching experience.

She expresses the following views about being a lecturer:

> *At its best an academic career is stimulating, challenging and rewarding. At its worst it is limited by our administrative duties and financial restraints.*

She considers self-motivation to be a very important quality for lecturers as they are expected to work independently and professionally. She also confirms that creativity is a valuable asset when teaching art and design:

> *It is vital to be aware of the creative process and to be creative in the way you deliver information to interest the students.*

IT skills are essential to Amanda, as she teaches CAD as well as doing administration and other tasks almost exclusively on a computer. Technical skills are necessary when she teaches students how to print fabrics and she describes planning and organisational skills as 'vitally important'. She also requires interpersonal skills and says that to be a lecturer:

> *You have to enjoy working with people, all of whom are individuals and will respond differently to what they hear.*

FURTHER READING

Magazines and journals

Drapers
Times Higher Education

Websites

www.edexcel.org.uk
www.gttr.ac.uk
www.graduatecareersonline.com
www.jobs.ac.uk
www.qca.org.uk
www.support4learning.org.uk
www.tda.gov.uk
www.ucas.ac.uk
www.vacancies.ac.uk

Working for yourself

There are two main methods of working for yourself: running a business or working freelance. There are many similarities between them and it is possible to combine both. Many designers aspire to working for themselves, pursuing their creative freedom by producing innovative, inspired collections without being restricted by an authoritative employer. With this freedom come many responsibilities and additional work, which it is important to be aware of before launching a company. To be financially viable, all businesses require customers so people who work for themselves need to establish, maintain and potentially expand a client base by offering products or services for which there is a demand. Business owners need to promote and sell their products or services or appoint an agent to do so on their behalf.

Being self-employed is a notion which is very much compatible with the way the fashion and textiles industry operates and consequently it is a popular option within most of the fashion and textiles careers covered in the preceding chapters. The most significant piece of advice which many people offer to those setting up in business is to work for someone else first, rather than going into business directly after graduation. This is partly to acquire personal experience of how the industry operates but just as importantly, it is also to gain relevant contacts. All businesses need suppliers and discovering which ones are reliable, reputable and produce appropriate products of the right quality can usually only be attained from an industry insider's perspective. Placements are particularly useful for students to gain an insight into industry. Being employed within a company also gives people the opportunity to make mistakes whilst on someone else's payroll and to learn from observing others' mistakes.

```
                          INVOICE
Invoice Date:
Number:

From: (your name, address, telephone number, email)

To: (name of person who commissioned the work and the company
address)

(list of work done or number of hours worked multiplied by hourly rate
e.g.)

original print design                              £200
three colourways x £125 each                       £375

TOTAL COST =                                       £575

Payable by cheque to: (your account name)
```

Fig. 17.1 Example of an invoice sent to a client from a freelance print designer

WORKING FREELANCE

Pattern cutters (particularly at ready-to-wear level), sales agents, textile designers, fashion designers and illustrators frequently work freelance, sometimes in
addition to being employed full-time by a company. Freelancers tend to provide
services rather than finished products and can either work to briefs set by their
clients or produce a range of ideas to present to potential customers. It is also possible to offer a consultancy service by advising companies on specific aspects of
business. Freelance work usually consists of working on several short-term projects simultaneously, preferably including some regular clients. Freelancers are
paid at an hourly or daily rate and request payment from customers by invoice
after the work is completed (see Fig. 17.1). The appropriate hourly rate can be
established by asking contacts in the industry for advice and is usually higher
than an employee would be paid, though this has to compensate for not receiving holiday pay and other benefits of working for a company. Income from freelance work is often erratic with busy and quiet periods throughout the year. It can
be relatively simple to start working freelance, but it is essential to establish
premises in which to carry out the work, possibly from home, and ideally with
customers lined up at the outset. Freelancers are responsible for paying their own
tax and national insurance and must inform the Inland Revenue when they start
working in this way.

LAUNCHING A BUSINESS

The main methods of setting up a fashion or textiles business are:

- opening a shop;
- launching a product range;
- establishing an agency or consultancy (see Chapters 8 and 13).

As the world of fashion is constantly changing, it is possible to develop other innovative business ideas which could fill a niche no-one else has yet covered.

Legal forms of business

There are three legal forms in which a new business can operate in the UK:

- sole trader;
- partnership;
- limited company.

Sole traders essentially own and run the business individually, though they liaise with customers and suppliers and may employ other staff to work for them. A partnership means that two or more people run the business jointly. Typically, two designers may set up in partnership, though it is often advisable for one of the partners to have a business or financial background. It is more complicated to launch a limited company, which has a separate identity from the people who run it. Co-operatives are businesses collectively owned by the people who work in them. A franchise is an agreement which allows the franchisee to run a branch of a business set up by a franchisor who owns the concept and supplies the franchisee with products. The franchisee pays an agreed amount of money to start the franchise in return for buying into an established business concept.

Business advice and support

Business Link and other general business advice organisations are available throughout the UK. Two government-funded organisations for dedicated fashion and textiles business support are located in the East Midlands and London, as the industry has traditionally been concentrated in these areas. The Designer Forum and Portobello Business Centre offer specialist courses and advice for setting up fashion businesses. Nottingham-based Designer Forum offers services to its member companies and educational institutions nationwide comprising:

- a directory of freelance designers;
- a design resource centre with access to a variety of fashion forecasting publications and websites;
- a CAD bureau;

- CAD training courses;
- trend presentations;
- weekly business workshops;
- business space;
- business mentoring;
- student and graduate events;
- a graduate recruitment service;
- advice to schools, colleges and universities.

The British Fashion Council (BFC), sponsored by companies within the industry, organises *London Fashion Week* (LFW) and a *Colleges Forum* to forge links between HE and the fashion industry. They have published *Designer Fact File* and *Designer Manufacturing Handbook* to provide advice to ready-to-wear fashion businesses. The Register of Apparel and Textile Designers publishes a list of designers and technical specialists. For an annual fee its members can access its commercial library and receive information and advice on commissions, pricing, portfolios, protecting designs and working freelance.

Financing the business

Businesses do not usually make a profit within the first year so some form of finance is required to run them in addition to paying for the owner's everyday living costs. Funding can be sought from:

- family or friends;
- loans from banks or building societies;
- grants from charities or trusts;
- sponsorship.

Banks and building societies employ business advisers to deal with business loan applications. They often request a business plan from the borrower, for which they usually provide advisory literature, and a guarantor for the loan may be necessary who will agree to pay back the loan if the borrower is unable to do so. There are several opportunities for grants within the fashion and textiles industry, with many businesses competing for them. The Prince's Trust is a charity which can offer low-rate loans or grants to unemployed people in the UK aged 18–30 who have business ideas and have been unable to find funding elsewhere. The Prince's Trust's Creative Industries Initiative offers support to design-led businesses. Regional charities around the UK also offer support to business start-ups within their regions.

Accounts, tax and National Insurance

Self-employed people are responsible for paying their own income tax. Records of income and outgoings need to be kept by the owner of the business and the services of an accountant may be required to file the annual tax return. The newly self-employed need to register with the Inland Revenue to inform them of their circumstances and to arrange to pay National Insurance, entitling them to benefits such as maternity pay. VAT (value added tax) is payable by companies with a turnover in excess of £60 000 (2005–2006).

Cashflow

Managing cashflow effectively is one of the most significant factors in running a business successfully. Fashion and textiles companies are particularly susceptible to problems with cashflow as the research and development for products takes place several months ahead of their subsequent production and delivery to the customer. Due to this lengthy process companies producing their own ranges can wait months before the investment in development is paid for by retailers. An apparently successful business which is attaining high press coverage and sales can struggle because of delays in payment. Most businesses need to pay for some form of insurance, e.g. for premises, products and public liability. Invoices are usually sent to customers after the goods have been delivered. The invoice shown in Fig. 17.1 shows a basic format which can be adapted for any business. It is important to include payment terms to state how soon the bill must be paid, typically within 28 days. Payment terms can be used to encourage customers to pay promptly by offering a discount if the bill is paid on time (e.g. 10 per cent within seven days) or being penalised if it is late (e.g. an additional 5 per cent after 28 days). The value of receiving prompt payment to someone who is self-employed is usually worth offering a discount.

Consultancy or lecturing

Having a regular second source of income can be beneficial to those who are self-employed to offset the unpredictable nature of business cashflow and this can be provided by earnings from consultancy or lecturing part-time. It is noteworthy that the three businesses discussed in this chapter have each benefited from this additional income. Visiting lecturers with current experience in industry are sought after by most fashion and textiles courses and lecturing hours can vary from a regular weekly slot to a one-off visiting lecture or project briefing. It is possible to find out whether appropriate part-time lecturing hours are available by sending a CV and covering letter to course leaders or heads of department in universities and colleges (see Chapter 16).

Sponsorship

It is possible to win sponsorship to set up a fashion or textiles business, though this is restricted to an exceptional few individuals. Texprint is a competition sponsored by numerous fashion and textiles companies to seek talented textile design students (see Fig. 17.2). Finalists receive the opportunity to display their work in

Fig. 17.2 Texprint First View exhibition in London 2005
Courtesy of Texprint. Photo by James McCauley

London, at *Indigo* in Paris, mentoring from within the industry and prizes for colour, print, knit and weave. Five winners travel to Hong Kong to *Interstoff Asia*.

River Island currently award £20000 to the designer of the most outstanding collection at *Graduate Fashion Week* and there are other prizes available at the event in fashion promotion and media. Fashion Fringe was launched in 2004, offering the winner a prize of £100000 worth of business support. Four finalists are selected annually by a panel of designers, buyers, journalists and academics. The finalists who 'can deliver an experimental, progressive and truly alternative approach to fashion' are given two months in which they receive funding, premises and technical support to develop their own collections which are shown during LFW. The project's founder Colin McDowell explains the need for Fashion Fringe on the organisation's website:

> *Although London fashion has generally been considered innovative, young designers have often failed because of lack of experience and technical knowledge.*

Organised by the BFC, 'New Generation' is a competition currently sponsored by Topshop and the prize is a fashion show and stand at *LFW* for up to three seasons, which helped to launch the careers of Julien Macdonald and Sophia Kokosalaki. 'Fashion East' is a non-profit project which runs off-schedule fashion shows at the Old Truman Brewery during *LFW*, offering a free show, PR support and £5000 each to three winning designers. American Express launched 'Business Express' in 2005 to provide business advice and mentoring for the winner from key industry figures: Topshop Brand Director Jane Shepherdson, Alexander McQueen and Times fashion writer Lisa Armstrong.

Emma Cook worked for designers Donna Karan and Martine Sitbon before launching her own ready-to-wear business in 2000 supported by sponsorship. Here, she explains some of the financial considerations of running her company:

> *I initially produced my garments at home then set up a small studio with a view to showing at* LFW. *I applied for and won New Generation sponsorship for three seasons to get the business going. There's no way you'd make enough sales in the first few seasons to cover the costs of a ready-to-wear collection, so you need additional finance*

other than profits, even if you've got sponsorship. A good way is to use your design skills for other companies so I've done consultancy work for companies including Harvey Nichols' own label and Ghost. The collection has a lot of press coverage and orders but you have to get the styles produced and in the shops – this is even more important than getting garments into the fashion show. I pay about £12 000 for my fashion show samples, which are outsourced to machinists. It costs me about £15 000 for a runway show and I have a free venue, but the average at LFW for other designers is £40–50 000. I did a business management course at the Portobello Business Centre and in hindsight if I'd have done that before it wouldn't have been so difficult for me in the first stages. To be financially successful, a ready-to-wear business needs to have a long-term strategy plan that can be adapted each season.

ADMINISTRATION

Running a business necessitates a variety of paperwork, depending on the size and scope of the company. The owner of the business needs to make time for administration or employ someone to do this. The main administrative tasks required within most businesses are:

- invoicing customers for payment;
- ordering from suppliers;
- paying suppliers;
- paying employees, subcontractors or freelancers (where relevant);
- pricing the products or services the business offers;
- filing orders from customers;
- sending statements to customers;
- keeping a journal of the business's income and outgoings;
- chasing up late payments.

Standard documents for this purpose can be bought from stationers or they can be printed with the company's logo and details for a more professional approach.

CASE STUDIES

Owner of a branded lingerie company

Career path

Sarah Fisk runs her own business designing lingerie under her own label. She graduated in 2000 with BA (Hons) Fashion and Textiles/Contour. Her final year collection was spotted in the *Graduate Fashion Week* (GFW) exhibition by fashion journalist Hilary Alexander who selected it for a photo shoot in *The Daily Tele-*

graph. Hilary introduced her to the lingerie buyer from Fenwick of Bond Street, who then stocked Sarah's range. In a summer break during her degree course Sarah was offered a placement with fashion forecasting website wgsn.com (see Chapter 3) where she subsequently worked as an assistant on the future lingerie trends section for two years after she graduated. Sarah continued to develop and sell her lingerie brand whilst working for wgsn and now works for herself on a full-time basis.

Role and responsibilities

Sarah works mainly in her design studio in Leicestershire and sometimes employs students to assist her either part-time or on placement. She cuts the patterns for her designs and uses industrial sewing machines bought with the support of a loan from a local business fund, to make her own garment samples to show to buyers. When she initially launched the business, Sarah made some of the garments herself, due to the difficulties of finding manufacturers to make small quantities. She now places all of her production with a lingerie factory which she can rely on for the standards of quality and service she requires.

Sarah describes her job as 'ensuring the smooth running of the company' and carries out the following tasks in order to achieve this:

- sourcing fabric samples and trims for the new range a year in advance;
- finalising designs and sample garments;
- establishing prices for production garments;
- photographing and illustrating the range for press, sales and marketing;
- organising shows and exhibitions to sell the range;
- sales appointments with buyers;
- collating the sales and ordering components and fabrics;
- booking a production schedule with the factory;
- quality controlling the garments;
- checking that orders go out to retailers on time;
- invoicing customers, accounts, tax and VAT paperwork.

Sarah often works on two seasons' collections simultaneously, starting to design for spring/summer concurrently with checking the quality of production for the autumn/winter range. Her signature style is vintage-inspired feminine lingerie with an emphasis on co-ordinated prints and trims and she frequently incorporates Liberty fabric into her range. Her products are stocked in London in Liberty and Topshop's Oxford Street flagship store as well as Parisian department stores *Au Printemps* and *Bon Marché* and Henri Bendel in New York. Her designs sell by mail order through Figleaves and *La Redoute* and she also developed a range exclusively for Marks & Spencer in 2004 which was sold in the lingerie departments of their top stores. Sarah promotes her range and gains new customers by exhibiting at trade fair *Salon International de la Lingerie*, which takes place in Paris in January and *Mode City* in Lyon in September. She visits customers and looks at trends in London once a month and occasionally travels to New York. When asked what she likes best about her job Sarah replies:

All of it. I organise every aspect of the company including promotion. I design all press information and packs, all photo shoots and the exhibition spaces ... but the most difficult aspect is collecting overdue invoices.

Career advice

If she wanted to employ a graduate, Sarah says she would look for applicants with the following qualities:

They would need to be self-motivated and easy-going with good organisational skills. Technical knowledge is also important for developing lingerie, combined with creativity.

For anyone wanting to set up their own fashion business, Sarah offers the following advice:

Start small and keep small, the company will grow with you when you and it are ready. Don't expect to earn much for the first five years.

Freelance fashion designer

Career path

Nina Faresin is a freelance fashion designer working mainly for suppliers to mass market retailers. She graduated in 1987 with BA (Hons) Fashion and Textiles and started work shortly afterwards as an assistant fashion designer for garment manufacturer Corah, having seen an advert for the job in the local paper. In 1988 she became a fashion designer at Coats Viyella in Nottinghamshire, where she worked for 12 years designing womenswear then childrenswear for Marks & Spencer, progressing to the level of senior design executive. In 2000 she started working as a visiting lecturer and began designing on a freelance basis. (Parts of the former Coats Viyella group were later bought by Quantum Clothing.)

Role and responsibilities

Much of Nina's work consists of designing childrenswear for mass market retailers. She currently has two main clients in the East Midlands: suppliers to high street retailers working with overseas factories. She describes the major elements of her role as:

- research into given product areas;
- initiating new product ideas;
- sourcing fabrics and trims globally;

- liaising with clients and retail buyers;
- issuing garment specifications;
- liaising with factories;
- preparing market information reports;
- trend presentations;
- garment presentations to clients and retailers.

Nina develops ranges of design ideas aimed at specific retailers including schoolwear for George at Asda and Woolworth, which her clients develop and sell to the stores' buyers. She is also currently working with a small private company to develop clothing for people with health or mobility issues. Though this particular project is not fashion-orientated, it gives her the opportunity to design with innovative technical fabrics to a challenging brief. She usually works with each customer one day a week in what she calls 'a loose framework of days', but has to be flexible as appointments with buyers can conflict with her regular schedule and she has to prioritise their availability over her own to retain their business. When asked about the advantages and disadvantages of working on a freelance basis, Nina replies:

I like being my own boss, the variety of jobs, always having new challenges and the flexibility of hours within my control. Being freelance can make things easier if you have children because you can work from home and don't necessarily have to work during normal office hours. The ideal is to build up regular clients so when you're researching you're thinking about those particular customers. A drawback is that when you're freelance people can think you're available all hours so people sometimes ring me about work on Sunday mornings or when I'm on holiday. The hardest part is everyone wanting things at the same time; having to juggle several different jobs at once. Even with regular customers there are peaks and troughs in the amount of work they give me.

Nina travels to see retailers weekly, visits London every six weeks for research and goes to *Première Vision* twice a year to source fabrics. She begins her design research a year ahead of the season and also works on some products a few months before they are delivered to stores. Forward planning is required for her workload to be completed successfully. Being a visiting lecturer during term-time gives her an additional source of income. Nina describes the skills she considers to be important for a freelance designer:

It is vital to keep a continuous flow of communication with your clients, the factories and the buyers. Self-motivation is essential because no work equals no money. Creativity is key for a designer because constant newness and fresh ideas are essential. Computer skills are useful for some things that I do and essential for others: I use email and I've just been on a course to learn Adobe Illustrator. Technical skills are important too because I couldn't do my job without an understanding of pattern cutting and garment construction, even though I don't make my own patterns. Planning and organisation are vital for a freelance designer or you will drown. You need to be flexible with the ability to switch your brain between several different projects within a day and to make sure each client is number one priority.

Career advice

Nina was unsure of her job options when she graduated as they had not been covered within her course, so she would recommend students to find out about the alternatives before graduating. She offers the following advice to potential freelance fashion designers:

I'd definitely advise getting as broad an experience as possible in companies to start with because that allows you flexibility and makes you more useful to more people. When you are freelance you have no commercial, technical or logistics experts to call on so you have to rely on your existing knowledge. Also, most of the freelance work I'm doing started through the contacts I made while I was employed by a company who recommended me.

FURTHER READING

Books

McRobbie, A. (1998) *British Fashion Design: Rag Trade or Image Industry?* Routledge, London.
Whiteley, J. (2003) *Going for Self-Employment: How To Set Up and Run Your Own Business.* How To, London.

Websites

www.adviceguide.org.uk
www.dti.gov.uk
www.fashioncapital.co.uk
www.fashioneast.co.uk
www.fashionfringe.co.uk
www.inlandrevenue.gov.uk
www.londonfashionweek.co.uk
www.texprint.co.uk

Support organisations

British Clothing Industry Association (BCIA) (includes offices of: The British Fashion Council; Register of Apparel and Textile Designers; Textile Clothing Strategy Group (TCSG); The Industry Forum; British Footwear; British Menswear Guild; International Apparel; UK Fashion Exports Association; The Silk Association)
5 Portland Place
London W1B 1PW
Tel: 0207 636 5577

Business Link
Tel: 0845 6009006
www.businesslink.gov.uk

Designer Forum
69–73 Lower Parliament Street
Nottingham
NG1 3BB
Tel: 0115 9115339
www.emtex.org.uk/designerforum.asp

Fashionworks
c/o The Islington Enterprise Agency
Tel: 0207 460 5050
fashionworks.freeserve.co.uk

London Apparel Resource Centre
Tel: 0208 802 5555
www.londonapparel.com

Portobello Business Centre
Tel: 0207 460 5050
www.pbc.co.uk

The Prince's Trust
Tel: 0800 842 842/0207 543 1234
princes-trust.org.uk

The Prince's Trust – Scotland
Tel: 0141 204 4409

The Prince's Trust – Northern Ireland
Tel: 028 9074 5454

The Prince's Trust – Cymru
Tel: 029 2043 7000

Textile Centre of Excellence
Tel: 01484 346500
textile-training.com

Finding jobs in fashion and textiles

Securing your first job in the fashion and textiles industry may not be easy, but several strategies can be adopted to assist your entry into a career, to make you stand out from competing applicants. Consider applying the same amount of effort and planning into gaining a job as you would to gaining a qualification. It is unfortunately the case that applicants are likely to be rejected for most jobs for which they apply. However, interviews should be perceived as valuable experience in themselves and if you are selected to be interviewed this is a positive step in itself since it means that someone believes your background is suitable for the job.

It is not always essential to have a directly relevant qualification for many jobs within the fashion and textile industry, as explained in the 'career routes' sections of the preceding chapters. Exceptions to this rule are usually jobs requiring specific technical expertise, such as pattern cutting and fabric technology, which are currently highly in demand, though it is possible to gain this type of experience without taking a degree. However, as the number of graduates in the UK increases it is possible that there will be more emphasis on vocational degrees, giving graduates of such courses a potentially greater chance of successfully finding careers in their chosen field. Whilst a large proportion of graduates in textile or fashion design become designers, the majority are more likely to find careers in some of the other creative roles covered within this book. Staff turnover within the fashion and textiles industry tends to be relatively high with employees regularly moving onto similar roles in other companies or changing career direction.

Many of the jobs in this book are head office-based apart from the obvious exceptions of most retail management and visual merchandising jobs. The majority of UK retailers and fashion publications and many suppliers' head offices are located in London and most companies pay a 'London weighting' to account for the higher cost of living there. If you would prefer not to live in London it is possible to be strategic and see what types of job are available in your preferred location and gear your experience and qualifications to this area. Those retailers and suppliers based outside London tend to be concentrated in the East Midlands, the North West and Scotland. Most careers in the fashion and textiles industry include travel nationally or globally and there are also many job opportunities overseas.

The following recruitment methods are used regularly within the fashion and textiles industry:

- press advertising: fashion trade press, national and local newspapers;
- speculative letters to employers;
- word of mouth;
- internal vacancies;
- fashion recruitment agencies;
- exhibitions and degree shows;
- university and college tutors and careers departments;
- industry organizations.

PRESS ADVERTISING

Trade magazines such as *Drapers* have specialised sections for appointments. Employers often advertise vacancies themselves, and even if a current vacancy is not suitable, it is advisable to note the retailer's head office address and a name from the HR department, for future reference. National newspapers are generally used for senior positions or large-scale graduate recruitment, as advertising space is relatively expensive. Local newspapers have vacancies in the major fashion and textiles industry regions. However, most fashion and textiles vacancies are not formally advertised.

WORD OF MOUTH AND INTERNAL ADVERTISING

Word of mouth is an extremely popular alternative to press advertising and most employees in the fashion and textile industry are likely to be recruited in this way at some point in their careers. It is possible to hear about a post in another company from a contact who works there and apply before the position is advertised. Fabric or garment suppliers can sometimes act as go-betweens in this situation, as they usually work with more than one customer, and are ideally placed to be able to recommend appropriate staff. When a vacancy arises, the company may seek internal applicants by identifying suitable candidates for promotion. Some companies issue their own internal vacancy bulletins, so existing employees can be offered opportunities first, prior to taking the more expensive route of advertising externally.

RECRUITMENT AGENCIES

There are many fashion recruitment agencies specialising in design, technical and retail vacancies. Most UK fashion recruitment agencies are based in London and some have regional branches. These agencies often advertise numerous vacancies in *Drapers*, usually with a job title, location and salary, in which the employers may be anonymous. Employment agencies charge the employers, rather than the applicants, for their services. The agencies are usually paid on results, so their recruiters are strongly motivated to match applicants to jobs. Deals between recruitment agencies and employers are confidential and the agency is usually paid a percentage of the employee's annual salary by the employer if the individual remains in the job for an agreed minimum length of time.

Agencies usually interview potential applicants prior to putting them forward for a job, to assess them in an informal interview situation whilst discussing their skills and job requirements. It is advisable to register with several suitable agencies. Fashion recruitment agencies keep a database of those who have registered with them and contact people when vacancies arise, before forwarding the candidates' details to the company if appropriate. Many agencies focus on jobs that require three years experience or more, some at executive level only, but some offer junior positions for graduates. Some agencies use head-hunting tactics to find the right person for a job, by directly approaching someone with the right experience. The services recruitment agencies offer to applicants can vary but most give advice on interviews and CVs as well as feedback on interview performance. (Goworek, 2001)

Working in a fashion recruitment agency is another potential career area in which fashion or textiles graduates can work, requiring good interpersonal skills and a sound knowledge of how the fashion industry operates. Recruitment consultants are responsible for:

- finding new candidates by advertising and headhunting;
- briefing candidates for relevant vacancies;
- interviewing candidates;
- expanding the client base.

CAREERS SUPPORT IN COLLEGES AND UNIVERSITIES

Prospects.ac.uk offers a wide variety of careers advice for university students. Each university has its own careers department offering relevant resources and advice to students. Art and design careers advisor Linda Brown sums up some of the key strategies to help students find fashion and textiles-related jobs:

> *Network in a variety of ways – join an industry professional body, lots of which have members' directories. Go to trade exhibitions and shows – contact them in advance*

to seek admission. Go to as many events as you can that raise your awareness. Persistence pays off. Get as many placements as you can from year one in a relevant company, even if it's packing boxes or making the tea. Big names can be more accessible than you might think for placements. Go to careers events at your college or university. Undergraduates may be able to use careers facilities at other universities during the vacation. Prepare your CV and have it checked by a careers adviser before you graduate.

Some universities offer careers modules within the curriculum of certain courses. Some major employers exhibit at graduate recruitment fairs and conduct 'milk rounds' on-campus at key universities to promote careers opportunities within their companies. A national graduate recruitment fair is held annually in Birmingham. Several retailers participate in the *Careers in Retail* exhibition, which is usually held in London in November. Employers and recruitment agencies often visit degree shows held at universities and national exhibitions GFW and *New Designers* to spot potential candidates for jobs. Tutors on many of the best degree courses are contacted directly by employers seeking graduates.

WORK EXPERIENCE

Gaining work experience as a student is one of the recommendations made consistently by the interviewees featured in this book, which is representative of the viewpoint of many people within the fashion and textiles industry. Even in jobs unrelated to fashion and textiles it is possible to acquire and utilise appropriate transferable skills such as communication, teamwork and organisation. However, working in a fashion or textiles-related business is a particularly worthwhile addition to a CV. Many students need to work to support themselves, but it is worth working simply to enhance your employability after graduation. Work experience gives you the chance to see whether or not a particular job is suitable for you and *vice versa*. A four-year sandwich degree includes a placement organised by the university for up to a year, sometimes offering a salary similar to that of a graduate. Work experience for shorter periods is usually unpaid, though some employers offer travel expenses, but it can be invaluable as a stepping stone to your future career. Methods of finding work experience include:

- approaching contacts given by tutors, friends or relatives;
- being selected through a sponsored project or competition as part of a course;
- sending speculative applications to selected companies.

The National Council for Work Experience sometimes includes fashion and textiles placements on its website.

SPECULATIVE APPLICATIONS

It is possible to find a job by sending a speculative application to a company, containing a CV and covering letter. Employers can find this useful, as being approached by suitable candidates saves them time and money by not needing to advertise. Explain what kind of jobs you are interested in and what skills and qualities you can offer to the company. Ideally, various companies should be approached, as many are unlikely to have vacancies available at the time you write to them. Think carefully about which employers you would like to target and find out where they are located via company websites, stores and adverts. Aim high – you have nothing to lose and everything to gain by contacting a list of your favourite companies. It is advisable to contact HR departments, as they should be aware of all current and imminent vacancies. Wherever possible, write to a specific person within HR or the department in which you would like to work, otherwise you are unlikely to receive a reply. Recruitment fairs, trade magazines and directories from trade fairs are useful sources of contacts.

KEY SKILLS

Experience and qualifications are not the only factors which companies consider when employing staff, though they can be the main elements which make one CV stand out from the rest. Two key interpersonal skills consistently specified by the interviewees profiled throughout this book are teamwork and communication. Other skills frequently mentioned are:

- IT skills;
- planning and organisational skills;
- technical skills.

Gaining work experience and/or a relevant qualification can give job candidates a stronger chance of being employed in their chosen field. You can establish some of the skills required for the career you are interested in from the relevant chapter in this book, scrutinising job adverts, further reading and research. Employers do not necessarily expect you to have gained all of these skills at the beginning of your career. Evidence of qualities and skills in job applicants can be demonstrated through qualifications, experience and responses to interview questions.

CVs

CVs should be clearly legible and professionally-presented, on a maximum of two A4 pages. Paper should be of good quality, but not brightly-coloured, bearing in mind that it may need to be faxed, scanned or photocopied. The first page needs to be interesting enough to hold the potential employers' attention and make them want to read further. CVs should be adapted to suit the job or company. For example, if the post is for menswear, put your menswear project from college at the top of the list of course content. This extra effort could potentially be the deciding factor in gaining an interview. CVs should begin with factual details including name, permanent address, date of birth, phone numbers and email address. Employment and education details should then be listed in reverse chronological order, with the start and finish dates. Graduates should give a summary of some of the relevant subjects studied within the course, as well as the course title and educational institution, as employers are unlikely to be familiar with the course content. Mention the grades of your qualifications if they are particularly good (As or Bs and first class or upper second class degrees).

List any relevant jobs in fashion and textiles you have had, including placements and part-time employment, mentioning briefly your responsibilities and some of the main elements that you learned from each job. Include any additional skills or abilities, such as languages and driving licence, and interests at the end of the CV. State 'references available on request' or if there is enough space, add the names, job titles, addresses and phone numbers of referees, whose permission you have sought first. For graduates it is usual to include two referees, ideally one from the university and one from a company you have worked in. It is advisable to read at least one of the many useful books on CVs or information from the university or college careers department for further advice.

COVERING LETTERS AND APPLICATION FORMS

Many employers send out application forms for jobs which must be completed carefully and accurately before being submitted, as this is the first impression that the company has of you. You may be asked to apply in writing for certain jobs, in which case you should include a covering letter and CV unless specified otherwise – some employers now use only online application forms and recruitment literature. The covering letter should be concise, usually no more than one A4 page. You should state which post you are applying for and where you found out about it before briefly explaining how your experience, qualities and skills meet the needs of the job. Put your address in the top right-hand side and the employer's name and address at the top left-hand side. Write to a specific person or if it is not possible to find this out, begin with 'Dear Sir/Madam'.

INTERVIEWS

Many interviews involve panels of interviewers, usually including the line manager for the post and at least one other member of staff, such as a senior colleague from within the same department or HR. There are likely to be at least two interview stages, with the best candidates from the initial interviews being invited back for a second interview. Some large retailers ask graduates to undertake an aptitude test for entry level positions before they are invited for interview, e.g. merchandisers may have numeracy tests. Many employers use psychometric testing prior to interviews which can help to indicate a profile of the candidates' interpersonal skills. Some retailers invite graduates to participate in recruitment days called 'assessment centres' which include a range of activities. This enables the company to observe how individuals perform in practice, and allows applicants to demonstrate their skills, with the emphasis on working well within a team to solve a set task. Candidates may be interviewed within a group setting and individually at assessment centres.

The purpose of an interview is for the employer to assess applicants' suitability for a position in relation to certain criteria including personality, attitude and appearance. Equally, the candidates' aim is to find out whether the job and organisation is suitable for them, so appropriate questions need to be asked to ascertain this. You may have the ideal skills for your chosen career, but you will obviously not have chance to implement them unless you perform well enough in an interview to be offered a job. Interviewers are often surprised by interviewees' lack of preparation, particularly regarding research into the company and what the job entails. Candidates therefore need to convince the interviewer that they are very interested in the job by researching in advance. Self-motivation is one of the key skills required for many fashion and textiles jobs, and as it is not always possible to show this through qualifications or experience, the level of enthusiasm demonstrated during the interview, as well as the amount of relevant research, will indicate to the employer how well-motivated the applicants are. Liz Gilder, managing director of the clothing and textiles recruitment agency People Marketing, reveals: 'the best prepared candidates get the job, not always the best candidates'.

The following list offers a variety of suggestions to improve interview performance by careful planning:

- keep up-to-date with industry trends by reading trade magazines and websites;
- consider which skills and abilities the employer is seeking;
- read your application form and CV again before the interview as a reminder of the information you have given about yourself;
- plan and practise appropriate responses to questions;
- think positively, as you have been short-listed for the position.

Presentation at interviews

Presenting yourself appropriately is essential in the fashion and textiles industry as your appearance could be one amongst several factors which could make you the preferred candidate. You need to show through your choice of clothes that you are aware of fashion and selecting the right outfit can depend on current trends, the job and the company. If possible, aim to buy your outfit from a store or brand which is more fashionable and in a slightly higher price bracket than the company which has offered you an interview. Take care in choosing your accessories, make-up and hairstyle for the interview which makes you look both fashion-conscious and professional.

Effective communication during an interview

It has often been quoted that interviewers make up their minds about whether or not to offer a job within the first ten minutes of an interview. Research has shown that people tend to remember most the first and last things that they are told, so you should consider the effect that this will have on an interviewer, by making an impact with your first and last comments. You should ensure that any contact you have with company personnel such as HR or reception staff prior to the interview shows you in a positive light. As an interviewee, you will probably be expected to speak for more than half of the time, as the focus is largely on you and your suitability for the job. You also need to listen attentively and carefully to the interviewer/s. How you present yourself is as much about how you communicate as how you dress. Consider your body language during the interview, as this can be more important than your verbal skills. Try to achieve an open and relaxed approach, without coming across as too laid-back.

Ask relevant, informed questions about the company, but don't expect confidential information to be revealed to you. You need to be honest, particularly when asked direct questions, otherwise this will put you on edge, but be selective in your comments. Explain career gaps if asked, e.g. it is accepted practice for many students to take a gap year spent travelling and this can be used in a positive light to demonstrate planning skills and use of initiative.

Do not offer negative information about yourself. Interviewers may ask you to explain your strengths and weaknesses, so be prepared for this question. When planning your response, make sure that the list of your strengths is the longest. Ensure that amongst your strengths are relevant qualities and skills for the job, giving examples as evidence. Consider your weaknesses, and try to phrase them in a positive way so that they appear to be redeemable. During the interview, aim to use assertive and confident phrases such as 'I can' or 'I will', rather than vague phrases such as 'I think' or 'I feel'. Think of yourself as selling your qualities, skills, experience, qualifications and knowledge to the company.

Examples of interview questions

Interviewers tend to ask similar types of questions adapted to the job vacancy relating to the candidate's skills, personal qualities, qualifications, experience, ambitions, the job and the company. It is advisable to prepare possible answers, though it is best to respond to the questions without notes. Typical interview questions include:

• What interests you most about this position?
• What do you feel is your strongest achievement to date?

- What kind of relevant experience do you have for the job?
- Can you describe a challenge you have faced and how you dealt with it?
- What do you intend to be doing five years from now?

Questions to ask at interviews

Interviewers often ask candidates if they have any questions at the close of the interview, and you could prepare for this by asking some questions of your own. Only ask about the salary in the interview if this is an essential factor in your decision about taking the job. Write the questions down and refer to them if necessary. You could select relevant questions from the following list:

- Are you conducting second interviews for this job?
- When will I hear from you about the job?
- What opportunities are there for promotion and progression in this post?
- Does the job include any travel? (If so, where and when?)
- Do I have the types of skills you are looking for in this job?

After the interview

Employers have a wide range of approaches to interviewing, and may adopt a demanding approach to see how the applicant copes under pressure. If you don't get the job you were interviewed for evaluate the reasons for this so you will be better prepared for your next interview. The company's HR department may be able to give you feedback on the reasons and you can apply to the same company more than once. Your interview performance and background may have been appropriate but the person they employed may have simply been more appropriately qualified or experienced. Even if you are successful in your application it is not necessary for you to take the job if you have reservations and if the employment market is buoyant you may prefer to wait for something more appropriate. If necessary, seek advice from tutors, friends and contacts in industry before accepting a post. If you do secure the job you were hoping for, but discover that you don't like it, it may be due to the way that a particular department in a company operates at that time, rather than meaning that the role is unsuitable for you, so it may be worth applying to other employers.

PORTFOLIOS

A portfolio of work is essential at interviews for designers, illustrators and stylists but is rarely requested for most other jobs within the fashion and textiles industry. Be highly selective about the portfolio content to show your skills to their best effect with a range of media and work aimed at various market levels, tailoring the content to the job for which you are applying. Buy the best quality folder you can afford and aim to make a particular impact with the first and last pieces of work. A3 or A4 sizes are used most often in the fashion and textiles industry as they are the most practical and portable dimensions. Course tutors can advise students on putting together appropriate portfolios. Fashion stylists and journalists accumulate portfolios of fashion spreads they have participated in. Fashion stylists or students wanting to work in this area may undertake shoots either for free or with minimal payment to practise their creative skills and add the images to their portfolios with a view to finding paid work. Would-be textile designers, fashion designers, fashion stylists and photographers could collaborate on a shoot to provide an outcome to be included in each person's portfolio. Visual merchandisers can compile a portfolio of sketches, CAD images or photographs of ideas they have implemented. Fashion recruitment expert Vanessa Denza OBE offers the following advice regarding the compilation of work for an interview:

> *Your portfolio should be an overview of your career to date but note that anything over two years old should be kept to an absolute minimum. It is advisable to treat your portfolio as an ongoing project – constantly working on your own projects as well as including examples of work from your current role.*

SELECTING A CAREER IN FASHION AND TEXTILES

Reading the content of this book will, it is hoped, enable you to decide whether or not you wish to pursue a career in fashion and textiles. Many of these jobs contain elements of glamour, high financial rewards and worldwide travel, accompanied by hard work and long hours much of the time. Researching into the fashion and textiles industry before working in it full-time is extremely useful, but you cannot know for certain until you do a certain job whether or not you will enjoy it or perform well. Many of the skills listed in this book can be learned in the workplace, but others, such as communication skills, rely more on your own personality. It is not too early to start planning a career during the first year of a degree course (or even sooner), aiming strategically for work experience and relevant part-time jobs. Students should begin their search for permanent jobs at the beginning of the final year, with the aim of finding a job within six months of graduation. If this time limit passes without successfully gaining employment, it may be worth considering a wider range of more feasible job roles or potential employers. Careers in the more glamorous and well-known roles and companies are highly competitive and it is worth considering other positions in which you may have a higher chance of success.

FURTHER READING

Books

Middleton, J. (2005) *High Impact CVs*. Infinite Ideas, Oxford.

Websites

www.denza.co.uk
www.inretail.co.uk
www.peoplemarketing.co.uk
www.prospects.ac.uk
www.retailchoice.com
www.work-experience.org

Careers guidance

Graduate Careerline (0870 770 2477) Tuesday, Wednesday and Thursday, 3–8PM.

Glossary of fashion and textiles terms

Branded merchandise refers to products which have been designed and developed by a separate company from the retailer, and are sold under the brand name of the supplier. This applies mainly to middle-market products.

Colour palette refers to a selected group of colours used within a co-ordinating range of products. Colourway is the term for a colour in which a particular garment is produced.

Comparative shopping is research into comparable products available from competing retailers. Buyers and designers usually undertake comparative shopping at least once per season, either for their own reference or to produce reports to share with their colleagues.

Cost price is the price charged by a supplier to a retailer for a product.

Couture fashion is featured in catwalk shows, designed by couturiers based in Paris and sewn mainly by hand. Couture is the most expensive category of fashion merchandise, as it is individually fitted to each customer.

Critical path is the series of key deadlines for product development and production which must be met in order for a product range to be delivered to stores for a set date.

Diffusion ranges are garments produced by ready-to-wear designers at a cheaper price level than their standard ranges.

Directional shopping refers to trips for fashion designers and buyers to major fashion cities to provide inspiration and fashion concepts for future seasons.

Fabric sourcing refers to the process of contacting fabric suppliers to select fabrics for garment ranges. Designers, buyers and fabric technologists can all be involved in fabric sourcing, which takes place mostly in meetings with sales representatives from fabric suppliers, or at fabric trade fairs.

Garment sourcing refers to liaison between clothing suppliers and fashion retailers, designers or brands, with the aim of finding suitable sources of garment production.

Grades are samples of garment styles in a specified range of sizes, e.g. for womenswear this may include the standard size 12 as well as samples in the smallest and largest sizes which have been ordered.

Lab dye or 'lab dip' is a small swatch of a fabric selected for a garment style, dyed to a specified shade. Lab dyes are usually sent by fabric suppliers to buyers for approval before the fabric is dyed in bulk production.

Lead time is the total duration of time which elapses from placing an order to the delivery of goods. This usually includes production and transportation of the goods.

Mark-up is the difference between the cost price and retail selling price of a product.

Open-to-buy is part of the retailer's budget for buying stock, retained for purchases close to or during a particular season, after the majority of the range has been bought.

Overseas sourcing offices are used by fashion retailers to liaise with suppliers in other countries.

Point-of-sale (or point-of-purchase 'POP') refers to in-store promotional material, e.g. brochures and postcards.

Potential customers are those at whom a retailer aims its products, usually defined by lifestyle, income bracket and age.

PR stands for 'public relations'. Retailers, brands and designers use in-house PR departments or independent PR companies to contact the press to gain editorial coverage of the company's products in magazines and newspapers.

Range planning involves planning the number and types of products required within a range for a future season, taking into account predicted fashion trends and historical sales information.

Ready-to-wear refers to garments by designers who show their ranges at the seasonal catwalk collections in cities such as London, Paris, Milan or New York. Ready-to-wear ranges are less expensive than couture ranges, as they are not made to fit individual customers, but cost substantially more than mass market garments. (Ready-to-wear is also known by the French term *prêt-à-porter*.)

Spec. sheet is an abbreviation of 'specification sheet'. A spec. sheet is produced by a designer, containing a working drawing and details on garment make-up, fabric and trims, to enable a sample garment to be made.

Strike-off is the term used for the printing of a design onto a sample of fabric. Strike-offs are submitted to buyers for approval of colour before fabric is printed in bulk production.

Visual merchandising is the display and presentation of products within retail outlets.

Working drawings are technical drawings of garments, often called 'flats' within the industry. They represent the products accurately with realistic proportions (as if they were laid flat) with the aim of effectively communicating silhouette and design details.

Index